CAREERS FOR

CAR BUFFS

& Other Freewheeling Types

RICHARD S. LEE
MARY PRICE LEE

SECOND EDITION

VGM Career Books

Chicago   New York   San Francisco   Lisbon   London   Madrid   Mexico City
Milan   New Delhi   San Juan   Seoul   Singapore   Sydney   Toronto

Library of Congress Cataloging-in-Publication Data

Lee, Richard S. (Richard Sandoval), 1927–
    Careers for car buffs & other freewheeling types / Richard S. Lee, Mary Price Lee—
2nd ed.
        p. cm. — (VGM careers for you series)
        Includes bibliographical references.
        ISBN 0-07-141147-X
        1. Automobile industry and trade—Vocational guidance.   2. Automobiles—
Maintenance and repair—Vocational guidance.   I. Title: Careers for car buffs and
other freewheeling types. II. Lee, Mary Price. III. Title. IV. VGM careers for
you series.

HD9710.A2L433 2003
629.28'7'02373—dc21   2003053548

* *

For Carolyn and in memory of Thad.
For Charlotte and in memory of Ray.
With love.

2 3 4 5 6 7 8 9 0   LBM/LBM   2 1 0 9 8 7 6 5 4

ISBN 0-07-141147-X

McGraw-Hill books are available at special quantity discounts to use as premiums and
sales promotions, or for use in corporate training programs. For more information, please
write to the Director of Special Sales, Professional Publishing, McGraw-Hill,
Two Penn Plaza, New York, NY 10121-2298. Or contact your local bookstore.

This book is printed on acid-free paper.

Contents

Acknowledgments

··

We wish particularly to thank all the interviewees and other auto buffs whose names appear in these pages. Their stories have made this book possible and—we hope—enjoyable. In this respect, we especially appreciate the help given us by Robert L. Fulmer.

Thanks go as well to Bruce Kelvin, fellow car buff and good friend. Bruce suggested resources and traveled with us to interviews. We thank Bill Hough for suggesting we advertise for careerists in *Hemmings Motor News*, a great idea we had overlooked. It was a pleasure to incorporate into our narrative our favorite racetrack, Grandview Speedway, with the cooperation of owners Pat and Bruce Rogers and marketing director–track announcer Ernie Saxton. We appreciate Gloria Bowers's interest and input and John Hill's wizardry on wheels. Finally, we thank Bert Parrish and Wayne Brooks for aid and friendship.

Introduction

Welcome to Automania

·····································

Is the automobile the most significant invention of the twentieth century? It's hard to argue that anything else came close from 1900 to 1950. Even in this era of genetic coding and medical breakthroughs, global positioning systems and digital technology, millions of people around the world use their cars as gateways to personal freedom and often as extensions of their personalities.

For thousands, automotive admiration becomes something more than just a means of transportation; it becomes a passion. The respect for, knowledge of, and wish to own or work with a particular car, a group of cars, or fine cars in general, may transcend the bounds of ordinary people's reason. These passionate souls are car buffs, or motorheads, and they live in a state we call *automania*.

·····································

Understanding Automania

Automania is unfailing proof that beauty is in the eye of the beholder. While all car buffs and other freewheeling types have a greater love for autos in the abstract than the general car-owning public, things get scattered and very personal from here. One person's treasure is another's shrug.

These preferences arise from almost as many sources as there are enthusiasts, but most depend on one of two elements, often on both:

1. Individuality
2. Age

Almost all preferences—whether for a 1911 American Under-slung or a 2003 Mini—relate to individuality. One enthusiast may hanker for the car Dad owned—or, more likely, the one Dad couldn't afford. Another may want the newest driving excitement on four wheels. A third car buff may be drawn to the 1938 Cord or the 1940 Lincoln Continental because nothing made before or since looks as beautiful. The hand-built hot rod may express another enthusiast's automania as no other object could.

Age is a factor if our dream car dates from a particular year, whether 1938 or 1972. Among car buffs, vehicle age alone never used to be a reason for interest. Now, the fact that a car, however unsung in its day, has survived for twenty-five years or more gives it a degree of interest, however small. Some states recognize this by issuing special plates to owners of old cars. Car folk may argue that age alone is no cause for respect. Don't assume that age alone equates with appreciating value. But the aged, if otherwise unin-teresting, car may be affordable and possibly—given enough years—collectible.

Some cars that are treasures now were also exalted in their days—the great classics of the 1930s, for example, or Carroll Shel-by's Cobra 427. Others, not seemingly outstanding when new, have grown in stature with the passage of time, their styling and mechanical attributes contrasting well with what followed, such as the 1955 to 1957 Chevrolet.

Some car buffs indulge their love through weekend tinkering on a piece of automotive history—or by lovingly detailing their brand-new toys—as they labor in other fields. Others make part or all of their livings directly or peripherally from their love of cars.

The people whose jobs we describe in this book have found a way to earn money from their interest in cars. We hope this book can make the same happen for you!

How to Use This Book

Before you read further, please understand that, with a few exceptions, the careers we describe are not related to the automobile as a commodity, but as an object of affection. In short, these jobs cover the unusual aspects of automobiling. We don't cover careers such as auto mechanic or body shop worker—other career books describe these occupations in detail—and we just touch on careers in new-car sales, but we do describe several other, more unusual, careers related to new cars, such as designer and engineer, because information on these types of careers isn't found in the average career book.

The skills you need vary by the job. Some of the jobs featured in this book call for a single skill. You'll need meticulousness but not much business sense if you're working as an auto upholsterer for someone else, for example. Other careerists, such as auto restorers, are virtual Renaissance people; work skills, people skills, and business acumen must be present in the same individual.

Also, keep in mind the following while you're reading this book:

- Wherever we say "car" or "auto," we also mean "truck," "motorcycle," or even "farm tractor," for automania knows no bounds.
- Although many of these careers relate to older vehicles, lovers of new cars are equal-opportunity car buffs. They can make a living or supplement their incomes through their enthusiasms just as well as the nostalgia types can.
- Since many of these careers are part-time endeavors and/or involve self-employment, salary and earnings are hard to determine. In the cases of salaried careers, such as automotive engineer, the salaries prevalent for similar employees in other industries would apply and are provided where appropriate. For more information on a variety of careers, including training and educational information and salary statistics, look to the *Occupational Outlook Handbook*

published by the Bureau of Labor Statistics. You can find it online at www.bls.gov/oco.

Additional Resources

This book describes more than sixty careers for car buffs and other freewheeling types based on the experience and advice of those who have succeeded in these fields. You can learn much from their experiences, and we hope they will inspire you to do further research into your particular area of interest.

To that end, throughout the book, keep an eye out for mentions of associations and other key words that you can then look up online or gather more information about from your local library. Wherever possible, at the end of each chapter, we've included additional resources, including associations, magazines, museums, libraries, and interesting websites for you to use to research the varied and interesting career possibilities for car buffs.

We strongly urge anyone interested in automobiles from an enthusiast or business viewpoint to buy at least one issue of the monthly magazine *Hemmings Motor News* (www.hemmings.com). It is far and away the largest and freshest resource, covering virtually all aspects of the field. A valuable reference publication is *Hemmings Collector Car Almanac*. It lists more than twenty-seven hundred car clubs, dealers, vendors, salvage yards, services, and people serving the auto hobbyist.

There are more than ninety other United States and Canadian consumer automotive magazines. Many are niche publications appealing to racing enthusiasts, Chevrolet Corvette owners, hot rod and street rod owners, and so forth. You may also want to research trade magazines that concentrate on specific areas of the auto industry, such as magazines dedicated solely to the design of cars and parts (*Automotive Design & Production*) or others focused more on manufacturing techniques. Visit the websites of publishers such as Oxford Communications (www.mediafinder.com) or Gardner (www.gardnerweb.com).

Another helpful library reference is the SRDS (Standard Rate & Data Service) *Consumer Publications and Agri-Media*, a book listing all consumer magazines. Every auto publication that accepts advertising is listed in Category 3, Automotive. This does not include auto club newsletters and similar private-subscription publications or catalogs. The leading consumer auto publications are also available on most newsstands and in bookstores; some can be seen in libraries as well as online.

With that, ladies and gentlemen, start your engines!

CHAPTER ONE

Jobs That Go "Vroom"

ehind every racing driver is a huge support staff. High-profile racing in any form is monstrously expensive, so there must first be a sponsor who puts up the money. Corporate sponsors hope to benefit from the publicity and product exposure generated by racing. Some sponsors pay the tab more for the joy of competing and the thrill of winning than for any financial reward. Next comes a racing team. This includes a director, pit crew, mechanics, timekeeper or scorer, and a staff to run the business end, which involves managing public relations and arranging the travel details. Some racing teams, such as the Roger Penske operation, even design and build their own race cars.

Sanctioning bodies exist to set the rules of racing and other forms of motorsports. These groups employ people in every area related to rule making, supervision, and enforcement.

Without racetracks, there would be no races. From the owner to the peanut vendor, each track is a business enterprise with its own hierarchy. In short, the race driver or drag strip top eliminator, while the center of attention, is just a tiny part of the giant industry called *motorsports*.

Racing Driver

For every Unser, Earnhart, or Andretti, there are thousands of unsung drivers—people who either make their livings or spend their dollars driving fast. But those not yet recognized must go a long, often arduous, way just to get behind the wheel. This doesn't include the weekend warriors who pilot their own wheels through sports car club races just for the joy of it.

Adam McMurtrie of Pottstown, Pennsylvania, "borrowed" his father's red Chevrolet one sunny afternoon and carved a circular dirt track from six acres of lawn around his parents' home. His father, a racer himself, punished his son not for taking the car or killing the grass, but for failing to wear a helmet. Adam was eleven years old.

Now, some sixteen years later, Adam McMurtrie is still racing only with more legitimate sanctions. His father, Charlie, now retired from racing, directs his son's career. The younger McMurtrie drives in Indy-style Formula Atlantic races all over the East, on the same tracks that brought fame to Mario Andretti, Roger Penske, and others. (Formula Atlantic cars are similar to Indy cars but one-third smaller.) Of fourteen Formula Atlantic events in which Adam competed in one year, he won or finished second or third in six. He won the first Formula Atlantic race he ever ran, beating veteran drivers on a rain-slick Pocono International Raceway.

Charlie McMurtrie operates an outlet business in Reading, Pennsylvania, and father and son jointly own two auto detailing shops and a car wash. These enterprises pay the racing freight, a costly proposition.

Adam followed in his father's racing tracks. Winning a dirtbike race at age ten was his first adventure on wheels, but he had watched his dad race everything from snowmobiles to formula cars, and he feels racing is in his blood. By age twelve, Adam was Pennsylvania and New Jersey's top-ranked dirt-bike racer in his age group. When he got his driver's license at sixteen, he bought an old car with money earned at the family car wash, gutted it, and campaigned on dirt tracks.

Alex Miller, a Sports Car Club of America regional racing official, thinks Adam McMurtrie is a natural, combining solid skills with winning aggressiveness. Adam's racing record shows that with experience and sponsorship, he may be ready for the next level: Indy-style racing.

Ready or not, the expense is daunting. Charlie McMurtrie estimated the cost of Adam's first Formula Atlantic race at $120,000, with each prerace preparation, including engine rebuild and setting up the car for the track on which it will run, coming in at $20,000 and more. But success can bring sponsors who are willing to foot the bills for the chance to see their names circling the course and hopefully coming to rest in Victory Lane.

The McMurtries have established a management company and now have several sponsors for their racing team. Adam McMurtrie may well become one of racing's household names. Father and son are surely working on it.

······························

Racing Publicist

Ernie Saxton started writing to publicize the famed Langhorne Speedway, now only a distant memory. He now writes full-time and has been writing columns for *Area Auto Racing News, National Dragster,* and the *Norristown Times-Herald,* a Pennsylvania daily newspaper, for more than thirty years. And for the past thirteen years, he's published *Ernie Saxton's Motorsports Sponsorship Marketing News,* an industry "insider" newsletter with subscribers in forty-nine states and overseas. He honed both writing and marketing skills with thirteen years as the marketing and advertising manager of Chilton Books, an automotive publisher.

In addition, Saxton does public relations and marketing for several national drivers and racing teams. Public relations is a catch-all phrase for a lot of activities. It includes promoting the drivers and teams wherever they're racing, publicizing their personal appearances at motorsports shows, and lining up marketing partners who will pay their share of the racing costs in exchange for representation on the race cars, in the accompanying publicity, and—if the sponsorship is generous enough—as part of the racing team's name.

These are not Ernie Saxton's only jobs. Midway between Allentown and Pottstown on Pennsylvania Route 100 is the village of Bechtelsville. Turn off the highway, drive up winding (and aptly named) Passmore Road, park in an open field, and you come upon what, in many people's view, is racing as it should be.

Grandview Speedway is cast in the traditional racing mold—a high-banked dirt oval with open-air grandstands, glorious summer sunsets over the far straightaway, and open-wheeled, boxy-bodied, roll-caged NASCAR sportsman-modified and late-model cars running four and five abreast. A Grandview start is one of life's great audiovisual experiences.

Ernie Saxton is this classic track's public relations and marketing person. This task involves churning out advance publicity to area news and racing media about each weekend activity in the April-through-October Grandview season. Another duty is publishing a forty-page souvenir program, the Grandview Groove, for each of the year's thirty-seven racing sessions.

"This is a tight track," Saxton says. "There are many qualifiers for each event, so you can have a big field, and that's always exciting. The place is a fan pleaser, and that makes the jobs of publicizing the events and announcing them very special."

Race Announcer

Although auto shows do not usually require continuous announcing, the person at the microphone must have knowledge of the new cars, the car show personalities, or the vintage vehicles that have won trophies in competition.

Unlike TV races with multiple reporters, most racetracks have single announcers. One person has the full burden of handling everything from local sponsors' public address system commercials to telling people what has just happened on turn three or what event is coming up next.

Race and show announcers have two traits in common, whether appearing on television or shouting over the roar of mud-slinging modified sports racers at the local half-mile dirt oval: clarity of speech and a thorough, instant, and accurate knowledge of the territory at hand. The first characteristic is more easily acquired than the second, but both can be learned. Training and education in the areas of broadcasting and communications can give you a solid foundation of skills on which to build as you pursue an announcing career. Ask your local librarian for more information about two- and four-year colleges that specialize in these areas.

If you're a Sam Posey, Jackie Stewart, or another driver turned television racing announcer, it's not simply because you've "been there and done that" behind the wheel that you are qualified to be on television. If you've raced at Indy, Darlington, or the Nurburgring, that's a great start, but you also must know everything possible about who's racing at your track, who's hot and who's not, and the likely battle strategies of the various racing teams. You may have help from research "stringers," the Cliffs Notes compilers of racing, but it's ultimately up to you. Televised races are announced by broadcasting teams whose members share the responsibility and complement each other's knowledge. While it helps to have raced, it's not an announcing essential.

Racing Mechanic

"I got started in racing by butting in," recalls Jim Bartik of Allentown, Pennsylvania. Being a racing mechanic is not his day job. It costs far more than the prize money his racing team earns. But he loves it.

"I went to Lehigh County Vo-Tech [high school], so I'm comfortable around machinery and working with tools. I started hanging around the pits at Dorney Park [an Allentown amusement park] when they still had racing. I talked to the pit crew guys and eventually they started giving me the 'hey-kid-hand-me-this' and 'tighten-that-bolt' jobs to do. I didn't know much to start with—I learned as I went along—but I got to know a lot of people in local racing, and one thing led to another.

"One driver I worked with turned around and helped my brother, Terry, and I when we decided to get into late-model stock car racing at Grandview Speedway. He had a garage with space, and his advice on setting up a car helped get us in the ballpark.

"We had some successes, and we learned a lot. Short-track racing is interesting and expensive, especially when you're footing your own bills. You seem always to be short of sponsors. Also, late-model stock wins and prizes are far less generous than they are for sportsman-modified racing."

One winter, Jim Bartik lost his job. His brother Terry decided "it was the perfect time for me to be out of work," Jim recalls. "I had time to make tons of calls for sponsors. I became our team's PR person as well as mechanic." Finding sponsors willing to finance a local team for the privilege of seeing their names on the side of a racing car is "tough duty," according to Jim. "You can't just send out a proposal and sit back. You have to keep calling, keep asking, keep digging."

At one point, when they had lost their garage space and were short of sponsors, the Bartik brothers were going to quit. The car, with a chassis that had never worked quite right, went up for sale. Then, they were fortunate enough to be sponsored by Schaeffer's Family Restaurant, a local landmark, and sponsors began to come aboard.

Terry Bartik's driving won Grandview's NASCAR Late Model Championship for 1995, with 5,233 points to the second-place finisher's 4,637. Although the team won only two feature races outright, Terry's consistent performance earned them the championship on points.

Jim took honors in his own right. Not only did he earn Grandview's True Value Hardware Gold Wrench Award for the year, but he also was named True Value's Regional Award winner and went on to be honored nationally at the NASCAR Banquet in Nashville as the True Value Hardware Mechanic of the Year for 1995.

Jim and Terry have both found their niches in the racing world and have received thrills, joy, and recognition for jobs well done.

....

Racing Pit Crew

In a race such as the Indy 500, one second can spell the difference between Victory Lane and second place—a difference that can run into hundreds of thousands of dollars. Such races can be won or lost as much in the pits as on the track. The members of high-profile racing pit crews are as skilled in their jobs as the drivers are in theirs, and every member has a specific task.

In a major race, the crew chief, chief mechanic, and pit crew can try valiantly to solve a car's problem as precious seconds tick away and the odds for success drift further away. More often than not, the problem is too much for on-site repairs, and the car is retired. "Not so at a dirt track like Grandview Speedway," according to Jim Bartik, the racing mechanic for his brother Terry's NASCAR Late Model Championship car for 1995. "In our kind of racing, if you take a hit, it's almost impossible to get the car straightened out in time to reenter that heat. [Heats are short events leading up to the feature race.] The racing mechanic and pit crew will try to get things together for the consolation race, and, if the driver does well enough, that team is in the feature race, too."

This kind of pit crew is strictly volunteer. Each member has a job to do, but they all pitch in on whatever it takes to solve a problem. "We get enough people in the pits to work on the race car on a Saturday night," said Bartik. "Sometimes, we're a mite short at the garage on weeknights, so we wind up working late two or three nights a week to help us prepare for the next race."

Between races, Bartik gathers the crew to check all the car's bolts to see they're torqued to the proper tightness. They grease the car and repack one of the four-wheel bearings each week, so they all get redone monthly. They also flip the tires, so the driver always has the sharpest edge on the proper side to compensate for wear. Tires cost $125 each and don't last too many races. They have to be on the soft side to grip correctly on dirt. Too soft and they last maybe two weeks. Too hard and handling is tough, especially in the feature race when the dirt track is thoroughly dry.

"That's some of what a racing team does to get ready for each upcoming weekend," he adds. "During the winter, we'll rebuild a lot of the car—if we have the sponsors to help."

....

Track Operator

Grandview Speedway's one-third-mile clay oval track is carved from a hilltop site, one that provides a grand view of the Pennsylvania countryside. The story, a saga of American gumption, started in 1961 when Forrest Rogers used a small inheritance from his mother's estate to buy a 105-acre farm. Forrest's son, Bruce, worked for a paving contractor whose manager, Alfred Lupacckino, owned stock cars. Since Bruce was involved in racing, the two men spent every spare moment and lunch break talking about local competition.

Bruce Rogers' favorite racing team, the Pottstown All-Stars Stock Car Club, tried to reopen a dirt track in nearby Sanatoga, but zoning changes made this impossible. So Bruce and Alfred Lupacckino got the trackless club together with Forrest Rogers, and the seeds of a racetrack were sown.

The plan was for a one-quarter-mile paved, banked track. However, after ground was broken, the All-Stars' financing fell through. Forrest went ahead anyway, switching to a one-third-mile dirt oval. Bringing this dream to life called for selling off some of the farm's acreage. Forrest Rogers did much of the work himself, helped by family and friends. When it all came together and became a reality, Forrest's wife, Amanda, named the track Grandview to denote the panoramic vista from the hilltop.

The first organized race was run on a go-cart track even before the main track was completed. Bruce Rogers raced, running as high as third place before blowing his engine.

On the opening day in 1963, fans bought tickets from the back of a car and clambered up the telephone pole-and-plank grandstands. Early races were held on Sunday afternoons because the track had no lights. If events ran late, racing would be called on account of darkness. Lighting was put in place about a year later and the track was on its way.

Two years later, Forrest Rogers died. The family could not sell the track and decided to close it. But Bruce Rogers and a former driver, Jerry Stinson, had other plans. They leased the facility from Amanda Rogers, and popularity began to build. By 1970, the track had improved lights and sound, a steel guardrail, and other upgrades. The next year, Bruce Rogers bought out his partner. Today, the track is the dream fulfilled that Forrest Rogers did not live to see, a NASCAR-sanctioned Winston Racing Series track and one of America's thirty best short tracks, according to *USA Today*. The track now seats up to seven thousand fans.

In 1990, Grandview inaugurated its popular "Thunder on the Hill" sprint car racing series and began twice-monthly cable-TV shows, *Bruce Rogers Presents the Greatest Show on Dirt— Grandview Speedway*.

Today, Grandview is a not-to-be-missed area institution and still a family business. Rogers family members include owner and event organizer Bruce, assistant event organizer Kenny, general manager Theresa "Pat" Rogers (Bruce's wife), assistant general manager and secretary Tina Rogers Missimer, and secretary Colleen Rogers (Kenny's wife).

The family aspect prevails in two other areas: competitors and fans. Over the years, there have been twenty-nine father-and-son racing combinations and twenty-three brother-brother duos roaring down the Grandview straights and into the turns. Also, some of the larger racing families' leading members have competed at Grandview. A. J. Foyt ran his last dirt-track race there. Other legends who have circled the oval include "King Richard" Petty, Kyle Petty, Rusty Wallace, Pancho Carter, and many others.

As for fans, Bruce Rogers puts it this way: "We take pride in making an evening of racing exciting and affordable entertainment for all the family. We keep our grandstand prices as low as we can, so whole families can come out to see the races, buy food and souvenirs, and go home with something in their pockets."

Rogers says he stresses enjoyment, and this means attracting the kinds of enthusiasts who have a great time together and love the show racing teams deliver. "We want all our fans to have fun and come back."

Related Track Jobs

Many jobs are performed by people who are paid per day and others are full-time track staff. Some, such as firefighters and paramedics, may be volunteers whose organizations receive donations from the track for each appearance. Taken from the Grandview Speedway program, these are typical of the tasks performed at local racing tracks:

- **Flagger, assistant flagger:** Relay the start (green), caution (yellow), black (disqualified), red (stop), and winning (checkered) flag commands to drivers circling the course before and during a race.
- **Line-up officials:** Place cars on the track as handicapped.
- **Pit stewards and handicappers**: Organize racing cars in starting and restarting positions.
- **Scorers:** Determine and record the running positions on each lap and the finishing positions for each competitor in each race.
- **Security guards:** Handle crowd control.
- **Tech inspectors:** Approve cars in each heat or event for safety and adherence to track specifications before racing and after any accident damage.
- **Track crew:** Aid drivers of damaged cars in getting off the race course, control race traffic, prepare and clean the track.
- **Track officials:** In charge of overall racing events, dealing with rules infractions and ordering yellow or red flags to slow or stop racing or black flags to remove race cars for rules infractions.

Other track-related positions include medic, track photographer, communications and electrical crews, concession operators, and push- and tow-truck drivers to clear the track of disabled cars.

Last, but far from least, someone with an alert mind and flying fingers must keep the electronic message board glowing throughout the races with the latest scheduling information, sponsor names, and other news for fans.

There are auto race courses of all kinds throughout the United States. For specific information, consult a motorsports publication such as *National Speed Sport News* or the sports pages of your area newspaper.

Additional Resources

American Speed Association
203 South Heritage Way
Pendleton, IN 46064
www.asaracing.com
> *This impressive association offers more than just news. Check out the career opportunities posted online.*

Automobile Racing Club of America
P.O. Box 5217
Toledo, OH 43611
www.arcaracing.com

Autosport
P.O. Box 280
Sittingbourne, Kent ME8 8FB
England
www.autosport.com
> *Both a print and online magazine, this publication is chock-full of racing news.*

NASCAR
www.nascar.com
> *The NASCAR website provides fans with the most up-to-date information and racing news.*

National Speed Sport News
P.O. Box 1210
Harrisburg, NC 28075
www.nationalspeedsportnews.com

CHAPTER TWO

Design and Engineering Careers

U nlike those automotive careers that can be started at any time, designing and engineering are rarely pursued later in life. It's best to decide early in high school that you want to become an automotive designer or a structural, electrical, or mechanical engineer in the auto industry. It is essential that you have a firm grasp of the sciences, have a strong mathematics background, and be computer proficient. Today's designers and engineers work more with computer-aided design, computer-aided manufacture (CAD-CAM) and similarly advanced engineering and drafting programs than they do with conventional drawing and modeling. Engineers and designers must have bachelor of science degrees as the minimum job requirement. They must be cooperative and work well with others, since they work almost entirely in teams.

Designer

John Samsen is an icon in the world of automobile design. He helped create the original Ford Thunderbird and Plymouth Road Runner. Not only did he design and name the Plymouth Barracuda, but he turned out many more designs in a career that's going strong years later.

Yet Samsen, an artist and engineer, is someone who did not foresee a future with automobiles. He majored in aeronautical engineering at Purdue University. His degree led to a job at McDonnell Aircraft, yet aeronautical engineering work did not inspire him. It consisted of "one thousand engineers, all determining the number of rivets for a given area of aircraft skin," he recalls.

Restless, Samsen started sketching sports cars. An admirer suggested he look into auto design. He came close when he applied for a job as a design engineer at the Raymond Loewy Studio in South Bend, Indiana. His interviewer asked if he had ever designed cars. He said yes, but that he had not brought any of his sketches with him.

Overnight in his hotel room, he drew several original designs. The next day, the Studebaker Corporation hired him as an engineer. He often went to the Loewy studio, where he was being coached in the techniques of car styling. When his engineering supervisor at Studebaker realized that John was more interested in car design than in the engineering tasks he was hired to do, he let John go.

Intent now on becoming an automotive designer, Samsen approached Ford Motor Company. Although he had not gone through a design school, which is the norm, he impressed the head of Ford Division Styling, Frank Hershey, who hired him.

Like other successful people, John Samsen believes that "if you want to do something and have faith in yourself, you can get where you want." Samsen knew his goal early, cultivated his talent, believed in himself, and put his stamp on automobile design.

"You need what I call a 'fantasy feeling' about cars—a blend of reverence for past designs with forward thinking," he says. "You can convey an impression of excitement or speed by subtly incorporating symbols of the past in contemporary designs. Effects such as louvers and air scoops can be purely decorative or practical. Horizontal lines can accent length.

"I think many industrial designers can't always make the transition to auto styling or do exciting auto work because they lack a passion for cars."

Samsen moved on to Chrysler, and after twenty years there, he decided to begin freelancing. Today, he remains his own boss. He designed for Navistar International and several other vehicle manufacturers. He is now preparing illustrations of classic cars and marketing them at classic car auctions and on the Internet. The computer has given many innovators, including Samsen, a new and exciting way to display their talents. His technique emulates the styling studio drawings of earlier times.

To be successful in the field of automotive or transportation design, you need to possess a variety of skills, including the ability to come up with creative new ideas, a thorough understanding of a range of complex surfaces, and strong visual communication skills, meaning you can illustrate your ideas. In addition, you should possess a strong passion for design and the desire to translate your ideas into reality.

How do you get into the field of auto styling? Because this is a competitive field, auto design departments are looking for people with solid credentials. A bachelor's degree in transportation or industrial design is now required by most employers. Getting that degree from a top design institute is especially valuable. Among these is the Art Institute in Los Angeles, a source of talent for many automobile companies, West Coast customizers, hot rod builders, and accessories manufacturers. Pratt Institute in Brooklyn, New York, the Cleveland Art Institute, and especially the Center for Creative Studies (CCS) in Detroit, which turns out many first-rate automotive designers, are all well-respected schools. Although vehicle design does not require an engineering degree, schools such as these include needed engineering courses in their design curricula.

When applying to design school, you need to submit a portfolio of work that you did in high school or in other creative occupations. Specific portfolio requirements vary among schools, but in general most are looking for creativity and good design sense, as well as some relation to car design. Many students prepare their portfolios in their leisure time, while others have taken design courses in high school or general adult education classes. Your school of choice will inform you of the application requirements.

There are a variety of magazines on the racks for those who love to look at the curves of a well-built car, but the top two trade magazines for those truly interested in design careers are *Car Styling* and *Car Design News*. For more information, visit them online at www.carstylingmag.com or www.cardesignnews.com.

Women Shine in Automotive Design

Automobile design is becoming an equal opportunity career. Years ago, the few women in the field usually only designed auto interiors. Today, more women are on the design scene, and they are showing a flair for creating exciting exteriors among other areas of the car.

Automotive design schools are encouraging women to enter the traditionally male bastion. Although women are a minority in auto design programs, their place within automotive design is becoming more assured. Women are right out there with their male counterparts whipping up exterior designs and making automobile interiors comfortable and eye catching.

Women buy more than half the new vehicles sold in this country—another factor that may account for the increasing acceptance of women designers. And women don't want just cars. They like trucks, sport utility vehicles, and vans. They spend well over $65 billion to assert their tastes. Toyota reports that almost 70 percent of Celica owners are women. Women purchase more than half of Chrysler's Jeep Grand Cherokees. Women also favor luxury cars, buying 56 percent of BMW's 325i convertibles. Finally, they like muscle cars—Chevrolet Camaros, Pontiac Firebirds, and Mustang GTs.

Auto executives are finally awakening to the fact that women, to some degree, influence 80 percent of all automotive purchases. For car stylists, this is a call to arms. Not only are they interested in what women like now; they are trying to analyze trends and anticipate women's tastes five or more years ahead.

While women buyers are in the majority, women automobile stylists are clearly in the minority, but they make up in impact what they lack in numbers. Styling studio heads at the Big Three (General Motors, Ford, and Chrysler) believe women stylists are already having an enormous impact on auto design. With four-wheel-drive vehicles alone, their concepts are dashing, combining practicality with verve.

Although women stylists design for everybody, they also design with the woman driver in mind. Mimi Vandermoler, Ford's highest-ranking woman designer, headed the Probe design team. She feels auto companies must get more women into the field and put them where major decisions are made. She also believes the woman driver's special needs must be met. These include seats that accommodate the short skirt and let smaller women reach a car's foot pedals.

How did some of the prominent women stylists decide to make their careers in automotive design? For one of them, the itch began as early as age five.

Cecile Giroux, a multitalented Ford stylist, fell in love with the race car in a TV cartoon series before starting first grade. She presented her father, a Chrysler engineer, with her own rendition of the car and asked him to build one like it at his plant. He laughed at the idea, but years later, he was to remember this incident with chagrin as she made her mark in the rival auto company.

Before joining Ford, Giroux attended the prestigious Center for Creative Studies (CCS) in Detroit and majored in the school's transportation design program. While there, she showed her flair early by designing a way-out motorcycle. The CCS chair's assessment: "It was so macho it just blew the guys away."

Giroux spent several years in Ford's European design schools in Italy and England, honing her skills. In her case, the career path to automotive styling was as exciting as the career itself.

Giroux has some unusual thoughts about styling. She wants auto design to reflect nature. Her love of animals is apparent in her designs. The graceful movements of a horse are translated into the smooth lines of an automobile. Verdant, cool forest colors are a hallmark of Giroux's interiors.

Liz Wetzel, a senior designer for Cadillac, once thought she would be designing blenders for a living. As an art student at the University of Michigan, she majored in project design. Teapots and appliances were her forte, but a summer job at General Motors' Truck and Bus Group ended her product-design aspirations. She returned to the University of Michigan and concentrated on marketing and engineering. Wetzel eventually returned to GM and worked her way up to a design slot in the prestigious Cadillac studios.

Wetzel strives to understand the attitudes of buyers twice her age. "I'm designing for a specific market," Wetzel says about interpreting the needs and preferences of Cadillac customers. One of the areas she pays close attention to is the Cadillac interior, and it's no coincidence that the roominess and appointments are reminiscent of first-class accommodations on a jetliner.

Julie Geldelman Dolan works on Chrysler cars' ergonomics, solving "people puzzles," such as how passengers fit most comfortably into a car. She had elected architecture as her major at Michigan State University when she quickly realized that the field lacked kicks. She transferred to CCS and felt instantly comfortable with automobile design.

At Chrysler, Dolan designed the interior of the Neon concept car and captured top honors at the North American Auto Show in Detroit. The preproduction Neon was the ultimate "Lego" car— add, subtract, expand, reduce. This idea car even had removable seats that users could take to the beach.

As is so often the case, Dolan's extremist ideas were not used on the production Neon. She didn't mind this because these progressive ideas can appear years later when studio heads, production people, and the public are more receptive to them. Still, the aura of friendliness she worked into her designs was retained in the production Neon. The executives had "picked up some of the fun of it," she says.

....

Engineer

Automotive engineers plan and develop new or improved designs for automobile chassis (structural basis), engines, manual and automatic transmissions, all-wheel- or four-wheel-drive systems, antilock braking systems, climate controls—in fact, every operating system that goes into a motor vehicle. They also modify and test every part of every system and subsystem using computer-based development programs. After conducting functional and performance tests of the components they design, they analyze the data these tests produce in order to create a final design that is as strong, lightweight, and cost effective as possible.

Few automotive engineers are trained in more than one automotive discipline. Instead, each specializes. A body or structural engineer, for example, is skilled in metallurgy (metals characteristics) and knows how to create strength in an assembly through the shape and design of its individual parts as well as by knowing which alloy offers the best performance for the job to be done.

Other auto-based engineers may specialize in chemicals, hydraulics, or electronics. They may work exclusively in one area, such as brakes, gears, paints and finishes, or production-line planning. As you can see, there is room in the new-vehicle industry for engineers of nearly every type. Women are entering this field as well, but they are still in the minority.

A bachelor of science degree in a field of engineering, such as mechanical or electrical, is a prerequisite for any engineering job. Starting pay in the industry is approximately $35,000. Add about $10,000 a year for each subsequent degree; that is, an engineer with a master's degree earns about $45,000 to start; one with a doctorate, close to $55,000. As with designing, this is probably not a career to start late in life due to the time commitment involved with education and the rapidly changing technology now being used.

Additional Resources

For additional information on automotive design and engineering fields, investigate the following helpful resources.

Automotive Design & Production
192 North Main Street, Suite A
Plymouth, MI 48170
www.autofieldguide.com

> *This industry magazine presents information covering all aspects of auto design and production, including a calendar of events, the scoop on industry jobs, new products and technologies, and recommended books.*

Society of Automotive Engineers (SAE)
755 West Big Beaver, Suite 1600
Troy, MI 48084
www.sae.org

> *The SAE is an excellent resource for technical information and expertise used in designing, building, maintaining, and operating self-propelled vehicles for use on land or sea, in air or space. You can find a lot of information pertaining to jobs available, meetings and exhibitions, and professional development opportunities on the website.*

CHAPTER THREE

Jobs to Build On

I f ever an automotive career invites potential disaster, the job of auto builder is the one. Since the Great Depression of 1929, only a handful of Americans have launched auto companies that succeeded at all—and the best of these lasted only a few years.

The person who came closest to producing cars in quantity was Henry J. Kaiser, the World War II shipbuilder. He built the unexciting Kaiser, Frazer, and Henry J from 1947 through 1955—adding a dash of zing with the sliding-door Kaiser-Darrin ragtop.

Among those who crashed and burned in the attempt to become auto builders were wealthy sportsmen Lance Reventlow and Briggs Cunningham; neither was able to put a car on the street. Preston Tucker managed to build fewer than sixty cars in 1947. Tucker's struggle is the subject of the movie, *Tucker, the Man and the Dream.* Former Subaru executive Malcolm Bricklin and onetime General Motors golden boy John DeLorean both made cars bearing their names, but their ventures soon folded, many millions of dollars and few vehicles later. But this road is not all paved with tragic stories. In fact, there are some successes to be had, especially if your taste in building runs to the unique.

Auto Builder

If reverence for the result is the symbol of success, Carroll Shelby succeeded. He launched a road-racing career with a borrowed MG-TC and ended with a stunning victory in the Twenty-Four Hours of LeMans for Aston-Martin in 1959. Sidelined by heart trouble at age thirty-seven after eight years of freelance racing, the colorful Texan decided his next move would be to start a performance driving school. Buoyed by its relative success and by a Goodyear racing tire distributorship, Shelby decided to build a sports-racing car. Although his enterprises gave him a living, he lacked the deep pockets needed for such a venture. He had to find financing.

In 1961, he learned that A.C. Cars of England had lost the engine supplier for its sports roadsters. Bristol Aircraft stopped making its exotic D2 six-cylinder engine, and A.C.'s own engine was overweight and outmoded. Since Ford had been one of Shelby's racing sponsors, its performance folks told him of a new, lightweight 260-cubic-inch displacement V-8 engine. As an option for a Falcon model, the Sprint, this powerful engine would enhance Ford's go-go image. Shelby secured a car, minus engine, from A.C. and got a 260 V-8 from Ford. The resulting marriage, while far from made in heaven, was enough for starters. Shelby approached Ford for development money. The car, he said, would be the Cobra—a name that, according to some stories, came to Shelby in a dream. Dream or not, Ford wanted name recognition for its money. So every Cobra displays a sturdy emblem: *Powered by Ford.*

Ford reasoned that Shelby's racing reputation would hype sales of the 260 V-8 in its own cars, so they agreed to bankroll the first hundred Cobras. Shelby used Ford's development dollars wisely to reengineer the A.C.–Ford hybrid as only a skilled racing driver could. Over time, Shelby's engineers replaced many A.C. parts with stronger, better-performing units.

As Ford made other engines available—the 289-cubic-inch V-8 and the unsurpassed 425-horsepower 427—Shelby's team continued to refine the Cobra. Eventually, even the A.C. space-frame chassis became almost entirely Shelby's design. Only the aluminum body panels came from A.C. Cars, and Shelby greatly altered them.

Shelby made the Cobra 289 in racing and street versions. In racing trim, it dominated Sports Car Club of America (SCCA) "A" production events. The fire-breathing 427 dominated everything on the road. Even the street Cobras boasted few niceties. So as fabulous as the Cobra was and is, it was definitely not for the average driver. Shelby produced only 1,011 Cobras between 1962 and 1966.

These days, Cobra replicas and knock-offs are a mini-industry. And the real thing—when you can find one—may command six figures. Not bad for a car that in 1962 sold for $5,995 with the Shelby-pumped 289 engine!

Later, when Ford introduced the Mustang in mid-1964, Shelby saw another chance to build cars. Ford figured a second investment in Shelby would deliver ample showroom payback for its dollars, especially since the popular Mustang was to receive the transformation, not an exotic import. Shelby turned the eye-grabbing but not initially road-grabbing Mustang into both a racecourse competitor and a true Grand Touring road car, the Shelby GT350. This could only be done with Ford's backing and the race-bred engineering skills of Shelby's development team.

To build his first cars, Shelby took over Ford's San Jose assembly plant for two days. The line ran only white "2 + 2" fastbacks (two front seats and two folding rear jump seats). They all had four-speed manual shifts, black interiors, and high-performance 289 engines. Shelby's designers gave the cars custom hoods with practical air scoops to ram-feed air to the carburetors. They fitted special disc-drum brakes, added instrumentation, and installed wide wheels and tires. Reworked suspensions included Koni adjustable shock absorbers, a limited-slip rear that fed power equally to both rear wheels, and traction bars to control rear wheel hop on acceleration.

In six model years from 1965 to 1970, Shelby's plant at Los Angeles International Airport turned out nearly fourteen thousand Shelby GTs. A convertible, complete with roll bar, joined the fastback. Engine options included the 427, and automatic transmissions were offered. Also, in response to owner gripes, the cars leaned less toward Shelby's design and more toward the Mustang influence. Eventually, the Shelby GT350 and GT500 "deluxed" themselves out of business. But, like the Cobras, Shelby GT cars today command many times their original $5,000 to $6,000 prices.

Why did Carroll Shelby succeed as an automaker where the others failed? Development money, perhaps—but other would-be builders had financing, too. Racing skills? Decidedly. Also, not having to design his cars from scratch certainly helped. Finally, the high esteem in which people hold his cars gives Carroll Shelby a place alongside other greats of American autodom. Shelby's cars, like those of E. L. Cord and the Duesenberg brothers, are legends on wheels.

Now, years later, Shelby has revived the Cobra. He has always owned unused vehicle registration numbers for forty-six cars. In 1988, he built seven in California (price: $500,000 each). Now, he is building the final thirty-six Cobras, at the rate of three to five a year. He has the support of a Las Vegas auto museum and a workforce of prisoners from Nevada's Southern Desert Correctional Center. His uneven but electrifying success story has spanned for almost forty years.

Hot Rod Builder

Shortly after World War II, hot rods began as modified road cars, usually late Model B and early V-8 Fords and mid- to late-1930s Chevrolets. Engines were spiced up with special cams, heads, manifolds, exhaust systems, dual- and triple-carburetor setups, and other goodies that made them go. Fenders were either removed or replaced by custom fenders to accommodate custom wheels and fat tires. Exotic color schemes and flame jobs were part of these very individualized cars. Owners often raced them in secret, side-by-side, two at a time, usually at night, using one-quarter mile of road as the racecourse. The winner of each pair of quarter-mile runs would race the other winners until one top eliminator emerged—or until the police showed up. Sanctioned NHRA (National Hot Rod Association) and AHRA (American Hot Rod Association) drag racing emerged from the informal street competitions. Today's "street rods" are somewhat different from the late-1930s originals.

"I started out at age fifteen with more than the typical teen interest in cars," said Ron Gagnon, owner of the New England Rod Shop in Auburn, New Hampshire. "I was into early Camaros and other fast cars. I taught myself a lot of skills by watching others and trying things on my own. This got me into building and racing drag cars.

"At one point, I had between $30,000 and $40,000 tied up in a car that ran great for ten seconds in a quarter-mile drag race. But for that money, I figured I'd be better off with something I could drive on the roads. So I got into building my own street rods.

"If I was going to learn street-rod building," said this Manchester, New Hampshire, native, "I figured I had to go to California, so I did. I spent four and a half years apprenticing in a California chassis shop. I wound up doing every job, from fabricating chassis to sending stuff out for the shop's mail-order customers. I was working sixty to eighty hours a week.

"I figured if I could work these hours for somebody else, why not work them for myself? So I moved back East and opened New England Rod Shop. I'm always learning and teaching myself. A lot of the skill of building a street rod is common sense—that and a desire to learn—to take a problem and to solve it. If a customer wants something that's never been done before, I'll usually try it."

Today's street rod pays tribute to the hot rods of yesteryear only in outward appearances. A 1934 Ford chassis is not the frame on which a "1934" Ford coupe street rod is built. Only the newest, most advanced components are used.

Today's rod starts with a concept, something in the future owner's mind. For example, he or she may want a car reminiscent of a '37 Ford coach. Once the builder knows what the owner wants, then it's time for the builder to start asking specific questions, such as: How should it be suspended—axles or independent suspension components? How big should the front wheels and tires be? The rear wheels and tires? Tires, wheels, and suspension must be chosen early, since their selection sets the tone for the design of the fenders, if any, and for the spirit of the whole rod. But they're just the start.

"The owner and I create the design," Gagnon says. "I try to come as close as I can to putting his dreams onto the street in chrome, steel, and fiberglass. The choices we can draw on are unbelievable today. We go over catalogs and price books from a ton of street-rod parts and component suppliers. Does he want Halibrand knockoff wheels? Too costly? How about Cragars? What does he want for power? Transmission? Disc brakes? Is a Ford nine-inch rear OK? If not, what?"

Body style, paint colors, grille design, bumpers (if any), instruments, steering wheel, upholstery styles and fabrics, and any number of other minute details must be considered, explored, and finalized before the work gets underway. These are, after all, one-of-a-kind cars, and that's what owners want—individuality.

The results are not inexpensive. Most complete street rods cost $40,000 and up. Gagnon has two in the works in the $80,000 to $100,000 range. Customers with cars under construction frequently visit the shop to see their projects, discuss progress, and nourish their dreams.

Oftentimes, the hardest part about building a hot rod comes in facing realities. A rod owner may want it all: smooth ride with top handling, awesome power with silence—but every car, whether it's showroom stock or a one-off street rod, is a series of trade-offs. The builder's job is to try to deliver as much of what the owner wants as he or she can.

"I'll build whatever's ordered," says Gagnon. "With turnkey [complete] cars, I'll manage the whole project and do all the assembly and a lot of the fabricating myself. I'll also start with a customer's rolling chassis and build the body. I'll do project jobs, too, like fabricating stainless steel exhaust systems. I'm good at heliarc and aluminum welding, so I've gotten into refurbishing antique motorcycles and making race car roll bars. They're a nice change for me."

A builder may employ trusted outside people to do the paint and upholstery work according to his or her standards. This isn't because he or she won't be up to the job; rather, it's a question of the most efficient use of the builder's time. It can take three hours to prep and paint a panel.

Ron Gagnon has never advertised and rarely promoted. A feature on his shop in *American Rodder* (www.americanrodder.com) magazine brought in a huge volume of work, but mostly it's his previous customers who send new business his way. This field is built on skill, reputation, and references, so the better a person's skills, the more likely that the business will flourish.

"I have an eighteen-month backlog of projects right now," Gagnon says. "Nine cars are in the shop, including three turnkey projects. I work entirely alone and have since I went into business." He works a tedious schedule, but the outcome is the best advertising any business could want.

For more information on hot rods, visit the National Hot Rod Association online at www.nhra.com.

Mechanical Restorer

In Groton, Massachusetts, a crisp, barn-red building houses KTR Engineering, a shop that specializes in mechanical restorations. Its founder, John Geils, formerly of the J. Geils Band, and three other talented people specialize in engine restoration for exotics, especially Ferraris and Alfa Romeos. They prepare customers' cars for vintage racing, although they are choosy about whose vehicles they accept in order to avoid potential liability. They also service newer exotic cars.

Geils's respect for vintage cars is a family matter. His father was a member of the Classic Car Club of America and owned a 540K Mercedes and K-Series Lincoln. But his own interests lie more toward sports-car competition. This stayed with him through school (Northeastern University and Worcester Tech). Geils began buying, repairing, and reselling old Ferraris as a hobby. He further sharpened his natural mechanical aptitude by doing a basement rebuild of a friend's Ferrari engine. They both learned by doing, since older Ferraris did not come with repair manuals.

With his added knowledge and confidence, Geils rented some garage space and began doing Ferrari engine rebuilds and mechanical repairs full-time. He even hired a crew, and they stay plenty busy rebuilding unusual engines and dynamometer testing each one. He teaches all of his staff members "all that goofy Ferrari detail" and will eventually turn the work over to younger hands.

....

Vehicle Converter

Many companies across America custom equip vans and install hand controls for handicapped drivers. But for more than ten years, there was only one person in the United States who made a full-time career of converting left-hand-drive vehicles to right-hand drive.

This was not a start-from-scratch career for Al Johnson of Goffstown, New Hampshire. He had been in the auto business all his working life, first with a service station, then a garage, and later tackling the interesting challenge of building street rods and modified cars. A move to a new home and a business timeout led to his unusual career.

Although there are right-hand-drive mail trucks used by U.S. Postal Service employees for small-town and suburban deliveries, the nation's forty thousand rural mail carriers traditionally deliver mail under contract, using their own vehicles as part of the package. Because they are independent businesspeople, their vehicle costs are tax-deductible, but right-hand-drive vehicles, sought by rural mail carriers for convenience, were simply not available. The few made in America were for export only—not legal for domestic sale. Even now, only Subaru makes a few right-drive Legacies for the American market, and a Pennsylvania company is trying to copy Johnson's Jeep conversions.

"I had a rural carrier friend who was constantly complaining about keeping his old delivery car going," Johnson recalls. "He was tired of driving with the controls on the left and the mailboxes on the right. Knowing I did modifying, he wanted to buy a new Jeep and have me convert it to right-hand drive. We checked one out at the local Jeep dealer and verified that the frame had been drilled on the right for a steering box, and I figured it could be done. The trick would be steering. Was there such a thing as a right-side steering box and mounting bracket? The dealer and I checked the parts books, and, sure enough, we could get the parts. My friend bought the Jeep based entirely on my assurance that I could do the changeover.

"The first one was a lot of work—they're easier once you teach yourself. I had to alter the dashboard for the steering column changeover, move the heater from right to left and rewire it, replace the steering box with the right-drive one, and relocate the steering column. The good part was that the instruments were in a center cluster so I could leave them pretty much alone.

"My friend loved the Jeep and my changeover and showed it around. Next thing you know, I had a second one to do. Then the Manchester [New Hampshire] postmaster saw it and loved it."

Johnson's new business really took off when he ran an advertisement in the newsletter that reaches all rural mail carriers. "When the ad ran, I spent the next three days at the phone taking orders," Johnson says. He has had to advertise only occasionally since.

Johnson has converted more than four hundred Jeeps. He has had as many as ten conversion orders at a time and delivered sixty-seven in one hectic year. "There's nobody here but me, in a barn behind the house," Johnson says. "It really tickled me when an overseas buyer wanted to see the factory! What was I going to show him?"

Not surprisingly, business came in bunches from areas where he had sold one or two vehicles. "For instance, after one sale, I got nine more, all from around Lakeland, Florida. I've had about forty repeat buyers, too."

Johnson has sold a few vehicles to right-hand drive countries, but the obstacles to sales are considerable. South African import tariffs are 100 percent. In right-sided driving New Zealand, a converted American Jeep costs more than $60,000 with the vehicle cost, changeover, exchange rate, shipping charges, and import duties. "Buyers don't mind the expense," Johnson contended. "Down under, converted Jeeps are real prestige vehicles."

When he began, Johnson charged $1,095 to convert a CJ7, and either he or the customer could provide the Jeep. His parts cost about $500 then. Now, with the more complex Jeep, the conversion cost is $2,495, and the job takes him about forty hours.

Al Johnson found a need within a niche market and has made a successful career by filling this need.

· ·

Vehicle Restorer

Restoring is the act of returning something to its original condition. Since that entire area is a core segment of this book, it's a good idea to answer an often-asked question: "How and where can I learn to do body work, upholstering, engine rebuilding (or whatever part of being a restorer interests me)?"

It is not recommended that one learn to weld by trial and error. Welding should be taught by a skilled welder who not only teaches the basics of welding but also safety. Or, if there isn't a convenient technical school near you, places that sell welding supplies often offer seminars and training courses.

Body work is very time-intensive, and saving time is important. Paint and body shop supply expos are helpful in providing information on time-saving new products and materials. Exhibitors offer free samples, technical help, and hands-on experimenting. Paint and body materials are constantly evolving, so you'll have to stay current or you'll be wasting valuable shop time.

Penny Bates, proprietor of Olde World Restorations in Huntingdon Valley, Pennsylvania, is unusual in several respects. First, she is a successful woman entrepreneur in a male-dominated business. Second, although she will restore any vehicle, she specializes in Morgans, a highly individual, very British sports car. They constitute about 50 percent of her business, and she maintains one of this country's largest inventories of Morgan parts.

This one-time potter and slalom canoeist spends most of her waking hours doing everything involved in restorations, from frame-up total transformations to engine repairs and parts replacement. Entirely self-taught, she knows how to do everything, but she also employs capable help, which isn't always easy to come by.

Operating her own business was a long-term goal, since Bates saw it as her best way to erase the wage gap between men and women. She also prefers being her own boss, although it includes being her own hardest taskmaster. The path to owning her own business was unique and unplanned.

"I got interested in cars long before starting my shop simply because I wanted to deal from strength about getting my own car repaired," Bates recalls. "I refused to be ripped off, as women often are. So I started working in a service station. I stayed for eight years. Learned it all."

Starting her business was a huge leap. She took eighteen months of business school courses in marketing, accounting, and public relations before opening her doors. Building an inventory of tools and equipment consumed big dollars, and building a reputation for quality work took time. During her early years, Bates also traveled to New York for seminars taught by the American Women's Economic Development Corporation.

The hardest part of the restoration business is financing. She bills customers monthly for work done, but she pays her employees each week. "When clients are late in paying or run out of money, it creates real problems. Most people who want cars restored greatly underestimate the cost. My advice is to take a high-end guesstimate, double that, and go up from there. You have to expect the unexpected every time.

"It's also just about impossible today to buy an old car, pay for restoration, and make a profit when you sell. You nearly always invest more than you can possibly recover. So, you have to want the car, not want to turn a dollar on it."

Does Penny Bates sense a gender gap with her peers, clients, or employees? "At first, some restorers had a 'wait-and-see' attitude about me, but my customers never did. I guess that accounts for the two-year waiting list I have now. There have been times with employees, however, when I know they wouldn't speak to a male boss the way they have spoken to me. Fortunately, these are very isolated situations."

Despite the list of waiting customers, she tries to find time to appear at car shows, one of her more effective self-promotion activities. Depending on her schedule, she makes from two to six such appearances a year. "Even though we're busy, I have to let would-be clients know about us."

Restoration Upholsterer

There are auto upholstery and convertible top or sunroof shops listed in Yellow Pages across the country. Most of these install ready-made tops, sunroofs, and seat covers. Some re-cover car and truck seats from scratch or make convertible tops from the tired old ones. But few such shops have the experience or patience to do acceptable restoration work.

A restoration upholsterer must know sources of original-type materials for seats, door panels, convertible tops, and carpets. He or she must know where to buy and how to work with genuine leather and with period vinyl. Such an upholsterer must be able and willing to replace battered original material tuck-for-tuck, seam-for-seam, using the old material as a pattern. Stitching, done by skillfully operated sewing machines, must be flawless. As you might expect, such perfect upholstery work commands far higher prices than installing an aftermarket sunroof or factory-made convertible top, running up a set of seat covers, or patching a torn seat.

Additional Resources

American Rodder
Street Rod Builder
Buckaroo Communications
701 Arcturas Avenue
Oxnard, CA 93033
www.americanrodder.com
www.streetrodbuilder.com
> *These are two of several publications from Buckaroo Communications that deal with the world of automobiles. Learn more about the publications and employment opportunities on the websites.*

National Automotive Technicians Education Foundation (NATEF)
101 Blue Seal Drive, Suite 101
Leesburg, VA 20175
www.natef.org
> *NATEF is a nonprofit organization that evaluates technician training programs against standards developed by the automotive industry and recommends qualifying programs for certification (accreditation) by the National Institute for Automotive Service Excellence (ASE). Check out the website for training and certification information.*

National Hot Rod Association
2035 Financial Way
Glendora, CA 91741
www.nhra.com
> *This organization provides a wealth of information online about hot rodding as both hobby and vocation.*

National Institute for Automotive Service Excellence (ASE)
101 Blue Seal Drive SE, Suite 101
Leesburg, VA 20175
www.asecert.org

ASE's mission is to improve the quality of automotive service and repair through the voluntary testing and certification of automotive technicians. The website provides information about membership, educational programs, and national automotive-related news, as well as job postings.

Service Technicians Society (STS)
400 Commonwealth Drive
Warrendale, PA 15096
www.sts.sae.org

The Service Technicians Society (STS) is a professional society dedicated to advancing the knowledge, skills, and image of service technicians. STS is an affiliate of the Society of Automotive Engineers (SAE). The website includes industry information and job postings.

Society of Automotive Engineers (SAE)
Automotive Headquarters
755 West Big Beaver, Suite 1600
Troy, MI 48084
www.sae.org

The SAE provides information and expertise used in designing, building, maintaining, and operating self-propelled vehicles for use on land or sea, in air or space. The website includes job postings.

CHAPTER FOUR

Moving the Wheels

Buying and Selling

S elling is the lifeblood of the automobile business. It runs the gamut from awesomely expensive new-car ad campaigns to your own classified ad. Almost every enthusiast becomes a used-car salesperson at some time. Most auto salespeople sell commodity new and used cars. But there are many other ways of moving the wheels. This chapter takes a look at some of the more unusual sales career options available for car buffs, as well as traditional new- and used-car sales.

Auctioneer

An auctioneer and the support staff at an auction company gather car buyers and sellers together. At auctions, cars placed with the company are sold one at a time to the highest bidder. The auction company receives a fee for its services, usually a percentage of the vehicle's selling price. Cars are often sold with reserve, a minimum bid price agreed on by the seller and the auction house. If there is no reserve, the seller accepts the highest bid.

In exchange for its fee, the auction company stages the event in a popular location, often as part of an auto show. Heavy publicity assures a crowd of would-be buyers who may pay fees for the privilege of bidding.

Brad Wooley, of Brad H. Wooley Auctioneers, Inc., in Little Rock, Arkansas, is a second-generation auctioneer. "My father was an auctioneer for forty-five years—he still is—but I had no intention of doing the same thing. However, I worked at it one summer and found I loved it, so I went to auction school, and I've been in it ever since."

It is not easy to become an auctioneer, and once you are trained and licensed, competition for work is keen. There are auction schools around the country, many approved for veteran's training. Training usually consists of an intense two-week course. Candidates learn the basics of developing a chant; the techniques for proper breathing, speaking volume, and stamina; and the basics of contract law and ethics.

Your choice of education could largely depend upon the licensing requirements for auctioneers in your state. Many states that require licensing for auctioneers only accept educational credit from specific auction schools or programs. Often licensing boards waive the educational credits if an applicant served an apprenticeship under a licensed auctioneer. Apprenticeships can range in length from conducting a few auctions under an auctioneer's guidance to working for one or more years. Call your state government offices to determine whether your state has auctioneer licensing laws and educational requirements.

Auction school graduates also gain experience by working for a practicing auctioneer as a "ring man." His or her job is to watch the crowd bidding at an auction and to ensure no bidders are overlooked during the bidding process. This "ring" experience teaches auction school graduates the fine points of how things work on the auction floor.

This is far from the end of the auctioneer's training. Wooley passed his state test and was licensed by the Arkansas Auctioneers Licensing Board. He has also taken Certified Auctioneers Institute courses sponsored by the National Auctioneers Association. These college-level courses are taught at Indiana University one week a year for three years. Auctioneers must have a minimum of five years of auction experience before they can attend. Many other organizations within the profession also offer extension courses and continuing education to help advance an auctioneer's career and knowledge in the field.

Auctioneers cultivate much of their business by making contacts and building relationships with bankers, attorneys, and people within the court system. These areas are the source for most auctioning business unless one runs an auction house and takes goods on consignment.

A good auctioneer will not let the owners get into the crowd and bid up their own goods to try to raise the price of the final sale. A good auctioneer will do his or her best to "talk up" the items being sold so they sound as appealing as possible and will work hard to get fair market value. The idea is to generate excitement and promote a sense of fun. The auctioneer keeps the bidding moving and tries not to give people much time to think about buying—the goal is just to have them bid.

"Having a successful auction is a matter of proper marketing," says Wooley. "We have to give every sale plenty of advertising and exposure so we're sure of having the right kinds of people—those who have a strong desire for the items being auctioned. We do targeted mailings as well as advertising. Our mailings go to people who have bought at our previous auctions, who have money, and who write good checks."

Exotic Car Dealer, Restorer, and Trader

Bill Hawkins has coveted Jaguars as far back as he can remember. Years ago, he began acquiring the high-performing Jags and other exotic cars, starting with a 1969 Jaguar XKE. His forty-car collection includes a Ferrari 408, a Corvette, a Maserati, and countless other specialty cars. He has now taken his passion for cars and focused his interests into two businesses. The first, British Restorations, is a shop he operates in Philadelphia. The second, a garage and dealership in Buckingham, Pennsylvania, houses an ever-changing group of desirable older cars. In addition to the vintage British cars closest to his heart—TVRs, Triumphs, Austin-Healeys, MGs, and, of course, Jaguars—browsers in Bill's shop will find a fine assortment of American boulevard specials, such as a 1955 Buick Century, and various muscle cars, including Plymouth Road Runners and early Mustangs.

Bill also sells what you'd call solid "daily drivers" or weekend hobby cars. He does not sell museum-quality cars, but collectible vehicles that people can have fun with and afford. These are complete, roadworthy, and often original, or well maintained, rather than restored.

Dealers often take cars on consignment from their owners, while the seller retains a portion of the eventual selling price as the commission. This allows the seller to operate a "showroom" business without the huge overhead involved in owning the stock on hand.

Bill keeps files on about three hundred available cars, for which he could earn a commission if he locates a buyer and brokers a deal. He functions as a car finder as well and says he can locate just about any model anyone would want.

Exotic car dealers require strong organization and research skills, along with a wealth of knowledge of specialty cars and their current market values. Buying interesting cars to repair or restore and resell is more hobby than career, but the lessons learned can be turned to practical use in the automotive field. Some who began as hobbyists, such as Bill Hawkins, have turned their talents to full-time business ventures, usually built around older autos.

Collector car prices started climbing in the 1960s and went through the roof in the late 1980s before sharply declining in the face of recession. During this time, it was possible to buy an older car, pay to have it professionally restored, and sell it at a profit in a rising market. Now, many high rollers who bought vintage cars as investments would lose a bundle if they were to sell their cars at today's prices.

The market is climbing again, slowly. Money can still be made, but you need a lot more experience to assure a profit. It rarely if ever pays to buy a car to restore; the better the car is to start with, the better off your overall experience is likely to be.

Whether you're buying a car for fun or gain, the beginner's rules
are the same:

- **Research the market before you buy.** Read local
  newspaper ads and publications such as *Old Cars, Special
  Interest Autos,* and especially *Collector Car & Truck Prices*
  and *Hemmings Motor News* to see which cars are
  commanding what prices.
- **Ask questions of old-car owners.** A good way to do this is
  to find a vintage car show and attend. Speak with the
  enthusiastic owners who love to talk about their cars and
  can provide some useful tips and guidance.
- **Know your budget beforehand.** Determine what you can
  pay for the vehicle and for any restoration. Get basic
  information such as hourly rates from several restorers as a
  benchmark; you can't get a firm estimate until the restorer
  sees the actual car and probably not even then.
- **Have cash ready.** When you go to see a car, this can give
  you leverage to make a better deal. But don't be rushed into
  buying something you don't want just because you have the
  money at hand.
- **Decide how much work to invest.** If you have the skills
  and tools to do some or all of your own work, you can bank
  your savings accordingly.
- **Have garage space.** You'll need this to work on your car, to
  store it, or both. This is essential for preserving what you
  buy and insuring it at the low rates for limited use offered
  by specialized insurers.
- **Pay a good mechanic.** It's always a good idea to have a
  professional check over any car you're seriously
  considering—even if you have knowledge of cars yourself.
- **Join the owners' club for the car you buy.** You won't find
  a better source of parts, technical aid, or camaraderie. (*Hint:*
  Join the club for the car of your choice before you start

shopping. Club publications are your best source of ads for the car you want and the newsletter articles will increase your knowledge beforehand.)

- **Schedule time for your project.** Otherwise it will never be finished.
- **Buy what's popular.** The type of car will depend on your preferences, but if you are buying to restore and resell, buy what's in vogue. Parts are more readily available, and more mechanics will have experience working on popular models.

Whether you do your own work or have it done, whether you take on a less costly "driver's car" fix up or an all-out "show-car" restoration, remember that the restorer's hourly rates (or your work hours) are the same whether the car is a classic or a dog. Remember, too, that a car starts needing restoration the minute restoration is finished.

Once the car is restored and ready to sell, there are some important guidelines to follow. First, advertise generously in local newspapers and suitable car magazines, including *Hemmings* and the car club magazines. Advertise months before you really need to sell the vehicle.

Again, research the market for prices. Don't advertise your car at the total of your costs plus an expected profit, but price yours with similar cars in similar condition. If the total of the costs sets the price of the car profitably, wonderful. But be realistic. Ask for more than you expect to get, but put a floor on your figure and try not to sell the vehicle for less. Above all, it is important to give yourself ample time to sell the car and avoid a position in which you must sell quickly.

It is also helpful to take your car to shows where prospective buyers can see it. Consider using a broker or having an exotic car dealer sell it on consignment for a percentage of its selling price. An auction is another viable alternative for marketing a high-priced car.

Broker or Locator: One-Make Specialist

Wayne Brooks of Bainbridge, Pennsylvania, has an interesting dual career. It has evolved and emerged from years of auto enthusiasm and vintage car ownership. A former airline passenger agent, Renault dealer, and exotic car repair shop proprietor, Brooks now leads an equally active but far different life. He is the American expert on Alvis cars and a broker and locator of these and other exotics.

It has taken years of painstaking work to build his computer databases, but Brooks knows who owns the vast majority of remaining Alvis cars in the world. Alvis built only twenty thousand of these fine British cars between 1921 and 1954, but an astonishing one-half survived World War II and the rigors of the road. Brooks learns of changes in ownership through worldwide correspondence and by reading ads in American, European, and British car magazines. He also keeps tabs on Alvis cars through the newsletter of the Alvis Owners Club, of which he is U.S. secretary.

When the largest Alvis parts supply warehouse was to be sold recently, Brooks spent months in England. His job was to see that the new owners got what they were paying for. He cataloged more than twelve thousand different Alvis parts by model, year, quantity, and interchangeability among models and years. (A few parts are common to every Alvis built.) As a result, Brooks created databases on Alvis parts and on Alvis cars and their owners.

He also keeps track, with his self-created databases, of where scores of other exotic cars are worldwide. In many cases, he knows almost all there is to know about these cars, including who wants to buy them. His searches often start with the would-be buyer.

Bringing buyer and seller together is the essence of Brooks's work as a locator and broker, but it's only the tip of his occupational iceberg. Most link-ups take a combination of subtle contact, relationship building, and patience. Quiet persistence is essential in contacting and negotiating.

Each transaction involves hours of planning and reams of paperwork. Sales between states can be tedious, and international transactions are infinitely worse. But through his hundreds of contacts here and overseas, Brooks can arrange everything from customs clearances to international transportation—whatever it takes to help a deal go through.

"My phone bill is horrendous," he says. Auto enthusiast magazines from around the world don't come cheaply, either (their classified ads are a major source of exotic cars). But as Brooks builds his network and keeps abreast of the volatile old-car market, his opportunities gradually increase.

He prefers not to act as a dealer but will buy an occasional car, often with a partner, if he must buy it to complete a sale. However, he usually has a buyer waiting for the car he locates. He still keeps one or two unrestored cars of his own to sell, but rarely more. "I can't afford to tie up money in them," he contends.

"Locating and brokering isn't for the fainthearted. You can't ever be sure a would-be sale will go your way. Temperaments, changes of heart, family objections, deaths, divorces, money problems, exchange-rate fluctuations, import-export snags, documentation hang-ups, missing correspondence—if one thing goes wrong, months of telephoning, negotiations, and paperwork can just dry up and blow away. But when something does go well, it goes exceedingly well."

· · · · · · · · · · · · · · · ·

Locator

Tim Chesher bought a 1967 Cougar and brought it to Buffalo, New York. It was rust free, and the original paint was in great shape. The response was tremendous, but the car didn't sell because people didn't believe it was truly rust free and original.

"Buffalo didn't work out, so we settled in Phoenix, where I did customer service work. The next year we planned a trip to Buffalo during my summer vacation. Before we left, I picked up a 1964 Chevelle in California that was really tops. The farther East I drove it, the more attention it got—but once again, nobody in New York would believe it was really original and rust free. So we started driving it back home to Phoenix.

"I'll never forget the one guy who did believe. He flagged me down in Fillmore, Indiana. He couldn't get enough. Here was the car of his dreams, in his town, for sale. He just kept circling the car, round and round, stalking it, almost. Of course, he didn't have the money—but he was so hooked he wanted us to come live with him until he could raise it.

"We couldn't do that—we had to get home. So with long faces all around, we returned to Phoenix. In a last-ditch effort, we drove another four hundred miles to a Chevelle show in Los Angeles. We didn't even enter, just parked it in the spectators' area—but won a trophy for the best unrestored [nonentered] car. And we sold the car at that show—for a $1,500 loss.

"I thought I'd have some fun with the whole misadventure, so I wrote a letter to *Hemmings* titled 'How I Spent My Summer Vacation,' and they printed it.

"That letter started my locating business. People responded, asking me if I could find rust-free Arizona and California cars for them. They were believers—just the opposite of the folks I'd met in my travels."

Chesher has been locating for five years and has moved from 300 to 350 cars. While not a staggering number, he has made money from the enterprise and enjoys what he does. "It's hard to get people's trust, but I've had no complaints about the cars I've found for people. I have repeat customers and people I can use for references."

People tell auto locaters what they want, and the locater acts as an investigator, reading ads and going to car shows in an attempt to find cars. When the locator finds a car that might be right, he or she takes pictures for the buyer, then reports back on the condition, odometer reading, and so forth.

It's the locator's job to negotiate best price and report it to the buyer, who wires the money, including a locator fee. Says

Chesher, "I never say I'm buying for someone else, and if I have to put a deposit on a car, I will do it first with my own money. Then I complete all the paperwork, arrange for shipping, and clean up the car. If it's a rare car and I can round up some parts, such as extra oil filters and a few goodies, I'll throw those in. I'll always have duplicate keys made for the new owner. I guess I'm hooked on customer service, even when I don't have to do it."

New- and Used-Car Sales

New- and used-car sales are still male-dominated careers, but they are becoming more open to women. In fact, one of the leading Rolls-Royce salespeople in the United States is a woman. This is only right, since women either buy or influence the purchase of more than half the new cars sold.

New-car dealerships are always looking for sales candidates. They often hire and train presentable but inexperienced people. The stereotypical image of the car salesperson as slick and untrustworthy is gradually giving way to that of a professional person, knowledgeable about the product and intent on meeting the needs of the buyer.

Payment is a salary plus commission, a commission only, or a draw against commissions. There are often perks, such as medical benefits and a new demonstrator car to drive. Some of the drawbacks include hours that can be long and a market that can vary greatly—along with the paychecks. Also, in the stretches of "floor time" between prospects, active but often frustrating cold prospecting may be required. Finding interested buyers and closing deals in a highly competitive environment can be harrowing, and there is little job security. A salesperson who doesn't produce after a reasonable trial period is usually let go.

Perhaps it's true that salespeople are born, not made. This maxim applies to Andy George, who is a sales consultant for a suburban Philadelphia Mercedes-Benz dealer. George combines his own sincerity and solid product knowledge with a studied appeal to a prospect's ego. He merges this ego appeal with the vehicle's ability to sell itself in a low-key presentation that usually works well.

On the test drive, George describes the car's high points during the first half, when he drives. After he and the prospect change places, George watches for reactions but says little. If George learns a prospect is interested in another make, he never bad-mouths it, preferring to emphasize the Mercedes' advantages. Half of George's business is from referrals and repeat customers, which he claims is the only way a luxury car salesperson can survive. He tries to be what he calls "good people." Evidently, it works. He has become friends with many of his customers and is on track to sell about 120 high-ticket cars a year. This keeps him busy because, in the fiercely competitive luxury car market, only about one out of five encounters results in a sale.

While the sales field does not always require a degree, many sales personnel possess a business or marketing degree, although prior sales experience and a proven track record can often outweigh any degree. A persistent yet pleasant personality is required for any successful salesperson, along with a strong focus on customer service.

....

Additional Resources

National Auctioneers Association
8880 Ballentine
Overland Park, KS 66214
www.auctioneers.org
> *Check out the website for more information on becoming an auctioneer.*

National Automobile Dealers Association (NADA)
8400 Westpark Drive
McLean, VA 22102
www.nada.org

> *NADA's mission is to develop research data on the automobile industry and operate training and service programs to improve dealership business operations and sales and service practices.*

CHAPTER FIVE

Auto Show Careers

There are both amateur (read "unpaid") and professional auto shows. Local organizations usually stage amateur or volunteer old car or street rod shows as charity events. A local hospital, for instance, may have a show on its grounds. The organizers offer plaques and trophies to the members of one or more local car clubs to attract cars and their owners. They promote the show with ads and publicity. The charity charges admission to the public and sometimes asks a fee of the car owner. In these shows, car club members may organize the event or coordinate the participation of their members.

There are paid organizations, too, that put public car shows on the street. One favorite is the "street show," staged by a professional show promoter for a town's chamber of commerce or volunteer fire company. The town closes a street to all but exhibitor cars, the public roams the scene (usually free), and town merchants and concessionaires more than compensate for the promoter's costs with added business on show day.

A new car show, such as the Philadelphia International Auto Show, involves everyone from a central coordinator or show promoter to the local dealer organization, the display and exhibit departments of the auto manufacturers (or the freelance display builders they hire), and the advertising staff of the area newspapers. High-profile vintage vehicle exhibitions such as Pebble Beach or the Concours d'Elegance of the eastern United States in Bethlehem, Pennsylvania, also use professionals to stage their car displays and judging events. These include advertising, public relations, and show promotion specialists.

Dealer Association Director and Auto Show Promoter

Bert Parrish has been executive director of the Automobile Dealers Association (ADA) of Greater Philadelphia since 1982. Over the years, he has helped the association grow from 33 dealers to 192. ADA has expanded its territory from central Philadelphia to the Delaware Valley, an area that includes the city and four contiguous counties in eastern Pennsylvania. Parrish has not only revived the Philadelphia International Auto Show, but he has helped make it a huge success.

"When I heard there was an opening for the directorship, I figured I'd give it a try." Parrish's only solid qualification was that he knew all the dealers and their managers from placing their newspaper ads every week as part of his job selling ad space and helping dealers write their ads for the *Philadelphia Inquirer* auto classified pages. "I'd been doing that for ten years. There were two of us applying for the job," Parrish recalls. The other man had a good bit of trade association experience, and Parrish had none. "But when I went before the dealer committee for my interview, it was 'Hi, Bert,' 'Hello, Bert,' 'How ya doin', Bert?'—and I got the job. I've been learning ever since."

As the ADA's director, Parrish assumed more responsibilities than he had planned for. "The job description was that of an office manager," he says. "I knew I was responsible for overseeing the annual auto show and staging a dealers' golf outing and dinner. But that was the tip of the iceberg.

"When I was hired, nobody told me about the politics I'd be dealing with, or the degree of support I would be providing for the dealer members. I learned as I went along."

As executive director of one of America's oldest auto dealer groups (ADA was founded as the Philadelphia Automobile Trade Association in 1902), one of Parrish's major duties is serving as an advocate for his member dealers. He often helps those wishing to expand their facilities, or to build new ones, in communities concerned with noise and pollution. Part of the job is to cite the overall economic benefits of a healthy and growing dealership to the community at large and to point out that the dealer is a good neighbor. "This isn't always easy. It may involve giving talks to the local Rotary or Kiwanis clubs, meeting with town officials, or helping my dealer state his case at a zoning hearing."

Another of Parrish's duties is keeping his dealers in touch with each other and with the causes and concerns that unite them. This he accomplishes through scheduled meetings, the annual dinner and golf outing, and a regularly published newsletter. He is also in charge of the yearly auto show. The Philadelphia show is traditionally held soon after New Year's—ahead of the New York Auto Show. One of his big jobs is getting manufacturers and their promotion departments to realize the importance of the Philadelphia show as one of their first opportunities to highlight new models and display advanced concept cars to elicit public opinion.

The show had been among the country's first, but it was nonexistent by 1968. It had stopped during World War II and did not have solid dealer support when it came back after the war. Parrish was expected to revive it within nine months of starting the job. Although ADA had hired a show organization to produce it, Parrish was ultimately responsible for the results. "I still am," he quipped. In putting on the Philadelphia show, Parrish, as the association's representative, has final approval of every show activity.

"My duties are to oversee every part of the production and coordinate our dealers' involvement." Since the manufacturers and dealers share the work and the costs, this takes a lot of careful planning. Parrish works with an outside show producer to complete all the steps needed to stage a major auto show. Within the show producer's organization are jobs such as these:

- **Executive producer.** This is the person charged with lining up factories and dealers and supervising the jobs done by all those at lower levels; in short, this person gets the show on the road, complete, and on time.

- **Talent producer.** Auto shows often include appearances by regional and national personalities from television, auto racing, and other sports. The talent producer works with the personalities' agents to arrange times and terms of personal appearances.

- **Advertising staff.** These are the people either within a trade show organization or from an outside advertising agency who create and produce auto show newspaper, television, and radio ads; dealer posters; handouts; brochures; and multi-page newspaper insert sections. The staff or agency PR people prepare news releases, arrange for TV and newspaper coverage of show highlights and appearances by any personalities involved, and manage a preshow party for the local press and VIPs.

- **Coordinating staff.** These people carry out all the details of putting on the show. They manage everything from planning the arrivals of exhibits from dealers and auto makers to seeing that things go smoothly between show staffers and convention center union tradespeople. In most show situations, union electricians, carpenters, and others must erect the light displays and knock them down after the show is over.

The Automobile Dealers Association of Greater Philadelphia is among those groups that support vintage sports car racing in a city setting. In recent years, the organization has also been one of many corporate sponsors of the Philadelphia Grand Prix, held each autumn. This two-day event features vintage auto races over a closed course in the city's Fairmount Park. These events hark back to the park races of the early 1900s. Other activities include new and vintage car exhibits, an auto art show and sale, auto accessories and parts booths, and marvelous spectator photo and video opportunities.

Model or Product Presenter

Professional models and product presenters are often hired as freelancers, or independent contractors, by auto manufacturers to participate in new-car shows. Unlike the attractive ladies of the past whose job was simply to adorn the new models, most of today's presenters do more than the automotive equivalent of Vanna White's letter turning. They are trained in the facts about the new car or cars they are highlighting with their good looks; then they present the high points of new models and answer the questions asked by show visitors.

Additional Resources

Extreme AutoFest
1565 Hotel Circle South, Second Floor
San Diego, CA 92108
www.extremeautofest.com
> Billed as an "automotive lifestyle supershow," this isn't your standard auto show. This shows hosts many competitions, in addition to featuring the latest cars, including street bike and car audio challenges.

North American International Auto Show
755 West Big Beaver Road, Suite 1100
Troy, MI 48084
www.naias.com
> This auto show, based in Detroit, dates back to 1907 and is one of the longest-running shows in the country.

CHAPTER SIX

Jobs Behind the Wheel

This chapter will cover those driving jobs that relate in some fashion to automotive enthusiasm. We are not discussing commodity over-the-road truckers, tow-truck operators, cab drivers, chauffeurs, limo or bus drivers, or similar driving jobs because you are likely to be familiar with these kinds of jobs already. Instead, in this chapter we describe driving instructors, performance-driving instructors, test drivers, drive-away drivers, and transporters.

Driving Instructor

A driving instructor is an employee of a driving school that provides driving instruction for compensation. Essentially, instructors teach others to drive. They often use dual-control cars, so the instructor can grab the wheel or hit the brakes if the student does something wrong. A calm demeanor, infinite patience, and cast-iron nerves are among the prerequisites. Instructors can be employees of schools such as those operated by the Automobile Association of America (AAA) or by entrepreneurs, or they can be their own bosses by operating their own schools. Licensing requirements vary by state, but the minimum is several years of driving experience and a valid driver's license with a spotless record.

In general, every applicant must meet these requirements in order to obtain a driving instructor's license:

- File an application with the state department of motor vehicles.
- Pay the required fees.
- Be employed by a licensed driving school.
- Be twenty-one years of age or older.
- Not be on probation to the department as a negligent operator.
- Have a driving record that does not contain a revoked license, an outstanding notice for violating a written promise to appear in court or for willfully failing to pay a lawfully imposed fine.
- Have a high school diploma or its equivalent.
- Have satisfactorily completed a course in the teaching of driver education and driver training acceptable to the department.
- Pass the required written and driving examinations.
- Have a valid driver's license.

A driving instructor license exam consists of a written test covering state traffic laws, safe driving practices, knowledge of the operation of motor vehicles, teaching methods and techniques, and regulations pertaining to driver education and driver training. In addition, applicants will have to take a driving test, which helps determine whether the applicant complies with all traffic laws and safe driving practices and tests the applicant's ability to give driving instruction. These roads tests are conducted in the same class of vehicle that is used for driving instruction.

Performance-Driving Instructor

The word *instructor* has a far more advanced meaning for Bob Bondurant, founder and extremely active president of the Bob Bondurant School of High Performance Driving. A racing legend himself, Bondurant draws his instructors from the top ranks of motorsports.

"Our driving instructors are all dedicated to motorsports. They strive to be the best they can be in the specific area that they're pursuing," Bondurant says. The drivers who apply to be instructors at Bondurant's schools have varied backgrounds, including motorcycle and off-road racing, carts, Formula Fords, Indy Lites, and Sports Car Club of America (SCCA) racing, among other areas. Where they have learned to compete is not as important as the quality of their driving, as well as their ability to teach. Many people are excellent drivers, but the same doesn't necessarily hold true of their ability to teach others how to drive.

When teaching people from all stages of life, including teenagers and stay-at-home parents and on up to some of the top people in motorsports, you need exceptional instructors who can teach at all levels of driving instruction. The Bondurant School employs drivers with proven track records who can communicate vehicle handling skills to others.

"The technology in today's car offers improvements in the areas of performance, safety, and protection," Bondurant adds. "Part of our job is to teach people to be better drivers by using the potential they already have but need to feel comfortable with. Our instructors know how to achieve this."

The Bondurant School has taught some of the best-known names in Indy car, NASCAR, Formula One, road racing, off road, drag racing, and boat racing. Bob Bondurant has also served as technical advisor on several motorsports motion pictures, and he has taught race driving techniques to actors, including Paul Newman.

After operating at Orange County, Ontario, and Sears Point raceways in California, the school opened its permanent home at Firebird International Raceway near Phoenix, Arizona, in 1990. The three-acre training center includes two straight-line slalom (cone negotiating) driving areas, throttle steer circle and skid pad, an offset slalom area, a handling oval, and a 1.6-mile road course. Some of the training exercises taught include accident avoidance, emergency controlled braking, autocrossing, skid control, and basic handling maneuvers. Garages, administrative offices, meeting areas, and even a museum are also part of the complex. The school has more than 150 race-prepared vehicles, including 30 Formula Ford race cars, plus Ford 5.0-liter Mustangs and various other Ford Motor Company vehicles.

More than ninety thousand people—from professional racing drivers to law enforcement officers, from teenagers to security-minded executive chauffeurs—have learned the fine points of driving at the Bondurant School. Instruction ranges from half-day courses, called FUNdamentals and offered exclusively to groups, to one-, two-, and three-day high-performance driving courses and four-day Grand Prix road racing. Each course has been designed to teach specific skills. The advanced road racing "graduate" courses must be taken within six months of previous Bondurant instruction.

Tester

Most automotive testers are newspaper and magazine journalists. The exceptions are the engineers responsible for the strength of preproduction vehicle components or for evaluating the total vehicle. When writers test, it is usually a combination of seat-of-the-pants (subjective) opinion and statistical (objective) information, compiled with the aid of engineering- or math-oriented people who record and calculate the test data. Thus, most automotive testers are people who drive for a living only to the extent that they write about their experiences; they are automotive journalists first and foremost.

Drive-Away Drivers

Although not typically a paying job, this is a wonderful way for people with time who love to travel by car to get where they wish to go at low cost. (The more people, the less cost.) It involves driving someone else's car to a specified destination. The availability of the car determines when the driver travels.

According to Auto Driveaway Company, a national organization, drivers must be over twenty-one, hold valid drivers' licenses with no violations, and pay a $250 deposit before each trip. The company refunds it when the driver delivers the car safely. Each driver gets a full tank of gas but must pay all other gas, tolls, and expenses. In case of an accident, the car owner's insurance covers it. Auto Driveaway authorizes up to $100 reimbursement for any auto repair needed en route. If repairs come to more than $100, the car owner must be contacted to authorize them.

Let's say you want to go from Philadelphia, Pennsylvania, to Miami, Florida. You would phone the local office of Auto Driveaway (in the Yellow Pages under "Automobile Transporters and Drive-Away Companies") and list yourself for Miami. When you receive a return call (from hours to weeks later—you never know), you'd pick up the car, drive it to Miami, and deliver it within a reasonable time. You would have made the trip for only the cost of your fuel, meals, and a minimum of motel stays. If others shared the costs but not the driving, you could travel in reasonable style, yet cheaply.

····················

Transporter

"My background is the home-moving business," says Frank Malatestal, president of Horseless Carriage Carriers, Inc., in Paterson, New Jersey. As a natural extension of my business, I started moonlighting in car transportation—including some I bought for myself at a museum auction.

"That went so well I jumped in full-time and bought the Horseless Carriage Carriers name with a few thousand dollars I'd borrowed and a promissory note from the owner."

From a modest three employees, his company has grown to one hundred people, building the business on word-of-mouth for being sticklers for detail and because people learned how careful they are with all cars. "I insist on spotless enclosed trailers, absolutely kid-gloves car handling, and holding to rigid schedules. Now we do it all: car transport, storage, even containerizing for shipping cars overseas and picking up or delivering to the piers."

Horseless Carriage now operates thirty trailers and does $4 million to $5 million in transport and related services a year. The company delivers all new Ferrari and Lotus cars sold in the United States, many of the Lamborghinis, and all sorts of classic, antique, and special-interest cars and trucks. It moves 450 to 500 cars a month, ranging from modestly priced cars to some of the world's most expensive luxury cars.

Horseless Carriage also transports a rare Rolls-Royce Silver Ghost wherever it is to be shown in the United States. "The driver who hauls the Ghost wears a suit when he loads, transports, and unloads that car. It's valued at $40 million."

Driver earnings are based on a percentage of transportation charges and depend on activity. Last year, one of the owner-operators earned well into six figures. Drivers for Horseless Carriage are owner-operators with commercial drivers' licenses. They must paint their own tractors in company colors and maintain them to Malatesta's exacting standards. "People say I'm crazy to be as fussy about everything as I am," says Malatesta, "but I have rules I insist on, and they seem to work."

....

Additional Resources

American Association of Motor Vehicle Administrators
4301 Wilson Boulevard, Suite 400
Arlington, VA 22203
www.aamva.org

> *This nonprofit organization represents officials in the United States and Canada who are responsible for administering and enforcing laws pertaining to the motor vehicle and its use.*

Auto Driveaway Company
310 South Michigan Avenue, Suite 1401
Chicago, IL 60604
www.autodriveaway.com

For more than fifty years, this company has served both private shippers and Fortune 500 companies, delivering trucks and cars nationally and overseas. Visit the website to find out how you can become a driver with the company.

Bob Bondurant School of High Performance Driving
P.O. Box 51890
Phoenix, AZ 85076
www.bondurant.com

The Bondurant School has graduated more than ninety thousand drivers since it opened in 1968. The website provides a list of program options as well as information on instructors and the driving courses.

CHAPTER SEVEN

Auto-Parts Industry Jobs

Without parts people, there would be no cars at all—let alone cars for racing, collecting, and driving around to the store or soccer games. The parts business is as huge as the industry that spawned it. Most parts companies are giant enterprises where being an auto enthusiast carries no weight; but there are exceptions, such as places where auto interest and knowledge can be turned into dollars by the entrepreneur. This interest and knowledge can be centered on meeting the parts needs of those who own one make and age of car (1940 to 1948 Lincoln Continentals, for example) or on marketing one kind of parts for many makes and models. It can put one or more skills to work, such as repairing one kind of assembly or replating parts from many years and makes. It can involve salvaging and recycling used parts for some or most vintage vehicles. It can mean reproducing one kind of product, such as rubber seals and molded parts for specific cars. For example, you could own a company that makes reproduction rubber window and windshield seals for most 1930s through early 1970s Fords, as well as scuff plates for 1933 through 1954 Fords.

All enterprising parts people share the following traits: a real interest in old parts along with the determination and skills needed to create or supply the demand for them.

Parts Locator or Dealer

"I've been a service advisor and service manager, mostly for Chevrolet dealers, but also for a Chevy-BMW dealer," says Patrick

Murphy of Spencer, Massachusetts. "I've been involved with cars all my life, and my interest falls into several areas."

Murphy says you need computer know-how to be part of auto service today, and those basic skills helped him develop a locating business for older Chevrolet parts. He's since expanded his home business to include other GM lines, plus Ford and Chrysler. "I trade mostly in NOS [new old stock] and reconditioned parts because I think used parts are too chancy.

"Over time, I've learned—largely by computer—which dealers and auto-parts stores still have NOS parts and accessories," Murphy explains. "One Western Auto store I found had forty sets of Foxcroft fender skirts from the 1950s in the original boxes."

Most dealers who deal in new old stock know it has value, and they keep it as long as they have space. But they usually don't have time to advertise and sell it. Murphy sees that as his advantage. "I know a good bit about who has what, and I can often supply what I'm asked for by checking the computer database I've built over the years. I advertise both ways, for suppliers and buyers, and that keeps my business going."

Most dealers price their stock fairly and still make a reasonable profit on what they buy and resell. Unfortunately, some unscrupulous dealers grossly overcharge for necessary parts. Likely their businesses won't last long because word of mouth among those in the know spreads quickly.

Parts dealers today rely on computers for their business, although they also go to swap meets and club events to buy and sell parts, accessories, and auto-related memorabilia. Dealers learn by doing when it comes to prices. They research the going rates to determine the resale values of various parts. Dealers build their knowledge of pricing for everything from Corvette emblems to early toys.

"You can use special-interest magazines and price guides, yes," Murphy explains, "but mostly you build up these layers of knowledge from your own experience and instincts. You have to teach yourself."

Parts Reconditioner

This career field usually involves finding just the right niche for someone with special knowledge of one particular part of an automobile. Someone with electronic and electromechanical repair skills might undertake a business repairing old auto clocks, speedometers, and other instruments. Skill in refurbishing old instrument faces would be an added asset. White Post Restorations in White Post, Virginia, not only does show-winning total restorations, but it also resleeves and rebuilds vintage auto brake cylinders—parts not easily replaced on many older models. The task includes disassembly and glass-bead cleaning of the old part, oversize reboring of the cylinder bore, pressing in a new brass sleeve, rebuilding and restoring the rest of the cylinder with new parts as needed, and finishing the outside, ready for installation.

Muneef Alwan of Oroville, California, restores original painted rubber or formed plastic steering wheels (original wheels are almost impossible to replace). The job includes filling cracks (nearly all early steering wheels eventually crack), priming, refinishing in the original color using ten coats of acrylic lacquer, high-gloss polishing, buffing and polishing stainless steel portions, or cleaning and polishing of chromed parts.

Several advertisers in *Hemmings Motor News* have turned their electronic skills with tubes, vibrators, power inverters, and other premicrochip electrical devices into vintage auto radio repair and sales businesses.

Plater

Chrome plating is a career that offers mixed opportunities. For a businessperson, it requires considerable investment in equipment—particularly with today's strict environmental protection regulations. According to Fred Hespenheide, owner of Paul's Chrome Plating of Mars, Pennsylvania, platers must be competitive yet quality conscious in a business that offers a future only if you focus on collectors' restoration interests. Yet for caring crafts-people, restoring chrome can be very satisfying work.

Chrome is not as fashionable today as it was in years past. Many older cars, particularly those of the 1950s and 1960s, were defined by the chrome they carried. They were truly works of art. People who are restoring those cars are the bulk of Hespenheide's auto-motive chrome-plating business.

Auto restoration chrome plating is not a batch business. It's dealing with one part at a time or several parts for the same car. Every item needs to be treated individually and with extreme care as many parts are irreplaceable. This calls for high-level craftspeo-ple at every stage: those who photograph incoming parts and write estimates; platers who prepare the old parts by reversing the plating process to strip them of what chrome remains; polishers who hand clean and buff each one while retaining its original design; and metalworkers who straighten bent sections of grilles and replace missing bars with new metal. It's demanding work, but lucky for Hespenheide, it's also in demand. It's also a trade he came by in an unconventional way.

Why is Paul's Plating operated by a man named Fred? Hespen-heide knew the original owner and saw that he was busy all winter long. So when Paul wanted to sell the business, Hespenheide bought it and retained the name. Paul's Plating has twenty-one employees, and 80 percent of the business is custom plating for show-quality vehicles. The rest is plating for motorcycles, boats, and other custom work. Paul's will even replate large pieces such as bumpers because many of the companies that once provided replated exchange bumpers have gone out of business.

"This is a business demanding skill," Hespenheide says. "We thrive on maintaining the lines and the sculpture of older plated pieces. With poor prep, the original quality of the part can be ground away or pitting can occur. We're proud of the letters we get from customers, and I'm proud of our platers, polishers, etchers, and quality-control people. They are real artists."

Replacement Parts and Materials Marketer

Fred Kanter, one of two brother-partner-owners of Kanter Auto Products of Boonton, New Jersey, explains how he and his brother came to this profession: "My brother and I graduated as engineers—I'm an industrial engineer, Dan is an electrical engineer. But right from the first, we saw buying and selling auto parts as something we could do to feed our car-collecting interest."

In the early 1960s, the Kanters were becoming pretty knowledgeable about Packards. At first, the brothers sold Packard parts as a hobby, but eventually they preferred running their own business to continuing in the corporate life. "At the start, we dealt exclusively in Packard parts, mostly NOS, and new old replacement stock [replacement parts made somewhat more recently]," says Kanter. "Later, we saw a need and diversified into hard parts for all other American makes and models. Now, vintage Packards account for only a small percentage of our business."

Today, Kanter Auto Products markets engine, front-end, electrical, brake, and other parts, plus accessories, for American-made cars from AMC to Zephyr. A few are NOS, but most are newly made as exact replacements for the hard-to-find originals. Theirs is believed to be the largest company in the United States that specializes in auto parts for vintage cars.

"We carry over twenty thousand different parts in stock," Kanter explains. "If we have a line—let's say front-end rebuild kits for 1938 to 1996 Chevrolets—we don't have exceptions; that is, if we stock for one model of Chevrolet, we stock for all models."

What began as a sideline to help the brothers enjoy their own cars is now a business with seventy-five employees. "We have 180,000 square feet of warehouse space—and guess what it's full of? Everything we couldn't sell. But we will, one day."

Car manufacturers don't make replacement parts for too many years after production, so as time passes, more and more cars become collectible, and, as more people start collecting cars as a hobby, keeping a variety of parts on hand will meet these needs. Kanter recognizes that adding entire lines of replacement auto parts entails a risk. "But so does getting up in the morning."

· ·

Additional Resources

Automotive Body Parts Association (ABPA)
P.O. Box 820689
Houston, TX 77282
www.autobpa.com

> *This is an active organization that is dedicated to bringing about better-quality replacement parts through certification, communication with and information supplied to state legislators and regulators, and representation of ABPA members on governmental and regulatory issues.*

Automotive Parts Rebuilders Association (APRA)
14160 Newbrook Drive, Suite 210
Chantilly, VA 20151
www.apra.org

> *APRA is an association of more than eighteen hundred member companies that rebuild automotive-related hard parts, such as starters, alternators, clutches, transmissions, brakes, drive shafts, and numerous other parts for passenger cars, trucks, off-road, equipment, and industrial uses.*

CHAPTER EIGHT

Careers with Accessories

ccessory is a catchall word for items the carmaker offers at extra cost on a new car. It also includes things that people outside the factories think the new-car buyer or older-car owner would like. Our definition also incorporates unusual auto tools—even apparel and racing souvenirs.

From the fuzzy dice of the 1950s to today's single-handed brake-bleeding tools, from exotic road wheels to double-jointed screwdrivers, accessories are as varied as the imaginations of the designers and inventors who make them.

Some items are the brainchildren of lone inventors who see a need and fill it. Others—especially add-on auto accessories, trim pieces, wheels, and wheel covers—are the creations first of designers and then of fabricators who turn the sketches and computerized dimensional drawings into final products.

Accessories Designer

In his column "Motor Matters" for *Auto Revista* newspaper, Vern Parker relates a story that could be titled "Finding Dad's Car." The car in question was a rival to Ford's Model A, the 1931 Plymouth. The fetching little four-cylinder is an attention getter even now. One of its engineering features, "floating power," consisted of hefty rubber mounts that isolated engine vibration.

Although drivers of the time may have admired the elegant "lady" ornament topping the practical radiator cap, few were aware that the pretty face and smooth ride were connected. Walter

Chrysler had wanted a design to celebrate his unique application. To this end, he approached an acquaintance, Avard T. Fairbanks, professor of sculpture at the University of Michigan, and asked him to design the ornament. Chrysler paid the sculptor with a 1931 Plymouth.

Over the years, Dr. David Fairbanks looked for the "floating power" ornament that had engaged his late father's talents. After being offered many badly damaged examples, he found a perfect "floating power" lady at an antique car show. The problem was, the ornament was attached to a complete car. Dr. Fairbanks wanted it badly, but felt the 1931 Plymouth Business Coupe cost too much. His wife disagreed—end of problem.

End of story? Not entirely. It was almost as though Dr. Fairbanks had found his father's car because the car he had bought had been driven just two thousand miles, and the owner kept it parked in his garage for the next fifty-nine years. Finally, it changed hands and was driven from Florida to Hershey, Pennsylvania, where Dr. Fairbanks bought it. Today, it reposes in Dr. Fairbanks's garage and still has fewer than eight thousand original miles, and the "floating power" lady is perfect.

Accessory designers today aren't typically artists or sculptors, although some may (quite rightly) argue their work is an art form. Today's designers are more likely to be engineers specializing in automotive design and focusing on one particular part of an automobile. Training in this area is similar to that of an automotive designer.

Other Designers

Tony Carlini's design talents have only recently turned to accessories. Carlini began custom painting motorcycles in a tiny building he named "The Candy Shop." Today, after creating hundreds of show-stopping Harley-Davidson Hog paint schemes, Carlini is marketing a biker accessory through the Motor Cars International mail-order catalog: a chromed paint-saver ring to keep creatively decorated (and just plain) Harley-Davidson motorcycle gas tanks from being chipped by gas filler nozzles. The chrome rings nestle neatly in place to protect any Hog tank when gassing up.

Boyd Coddington has designed and built drop-dead hot rods for rock stars and Hollywood nostalgia types at prices into the middle six figures. He also markets billet aluminum wheels as well as his custom-designed steering wheels for hot rodders and those seeking the ultimate custom wheels. These products are sold by mail from the California Car Cover Company. The road wheels start at $1,295 for a set of four; a Boyds steering wheel comes to $384 by the time one arrives at your door.

Mail-Order Merchant

One of the gurus of the accessories mail-order business—a West Coast specialist in exotic automotive tools, supplies, and auto novelties—revealed some interesting sidelights of this occupation but chose not to give his name.

"This can be a difficult, expensive, and chancy business, but if you know your market and your product and establish a reputable business, you can make a good living at it.

"I started my catalog sales enterprise based on what I learned in my career as a racing mechanic and instructor. I couldn't find the quality of automotive tools I demanded, so I went looking abroad. I got lucky in my search and reasoned that if I could use better-quality tools, others could, too. Well, they could, they can—and they do. But getting the word out and the orders in has been an experience."

Mail-order merchants build mailing lists made up of enthusiasts who read certain publications and people whose demographics indicate an interest in automotive quality as well as a certain income bracket. But with even the best list sorting, many mail-order catalogs generate orders from only about one-third of

1 percent of the catalogs sent out. With mail rates at an all-time high and the exchange rate changing, importing quality items while pricing them as attractively as possible and still earning a profit can be a challenge. That said, if you have a keen business sense and know your product and the demand of your audience, with hard work and determination, you should do well.

This particular vendor's mail-order catalog reflects his lively personality and his continual quest for excellence. "I'm not a trained writer, but I prepare every catalog blurb and have several versions of the catalog going out each year."

Think about the variety of mail-order catalogs you receive or find around the house or at your workplace. Look at the quality of construction and how the various items are arranged and displayed. Is there anything you would do differently? As a mail-order merchant, you would get to call the shots and choose which items to sell and how to feature them.

It's not all shopping and creativity, though: to make this type of business work, you also need keen business acumen. This is something you can develop by taking business and marketing courses at a community college or four-year college or university. Many courses are offered that can help you prepare to launch and successfully operate your own business. Contact a school career counselor at a college near you for more information.

Accessories Manufacturing

As a process, accessories manufacturing is similar to any other manufacturing operation. The fact that you're working in a plant that makes "aftermarket" (for existing vehicles) road wheels for auto stores to sell or sunroofs for auto top shops to install doesn't necessarily mean it's a job meant for car buffs.

The company now known as ASC is an exception. It began as American Sunroof Corporation in a small shop in Ann Arbor, Michigan, that made and installed sunroofs. Today, ASC operates on both coasts and in Europe. ASC does custom and production work for many automakers, including proposal cars and limited-production convertibles. Its corporate structure includes sales and marketing staffs as well as production workers of many disciplines. These are cutting-edge car buffs who approach their careers with innovation and excitement.

Accessories Retailing

Thousands of auto parts stores and a handful of automotive stores focus on licensed racing memorabilia, ranging from T-shirts and license-plate frames to Mustang leather jackets. They also sell models, posters, key rings, books, banners, caps, and videos.

As an owner of this type of store, you would be responsible for finding and maintaining your retail space, purchasing the goods, pricing and displaying them on the shelves, budgeting your profits and losses, advertising and marketing, and hiring and paying any employees that you might have. Being a small-business owner, especially of a specialty shop, takes a lot of hard work and dedication. The hard work and difficulty is often offset, however, by the pleasures of working as your own boss and calling your own shots.

Auto parts and accessories stores are owned and operated as any small business would be, unless it's a franchise. In that case, you must abide by the standards and business model of the franchise. There's more security in owning a franchise because you already have name recognition and don't need to spend as much time on publicity. With more security, however, comes less autonomy.

Additional Resources

For more information on entrepreneurial businesses and how you can create your own successful business in any of the areas featured in this chapter, check out the following magazines, websites, and associations for more information.

Catalog Success
Inside Direct Mail
401 North Broad Street
Philadelphia, PA 19108
www.catalogsuccess.com
> *This industry magazine provides case studies, how-to information, and advice from experts on a variety of topics.*

Direct Marketing Association (DMA)
1120 Avenue of the Americas
New York, NY 10036
www.the-dma.org
> *DMA is the largest trade association for businesses interested in direct, database, and interactive global marketing. The website offers advice and information on a range of topics and includes postings for conferences, seminars, and contact information for local chapters.*

Entrepreneur.com
Entrepreneur Media Inc.
2445 McCabe Way
Irvine, CA 92614
www.entrepreneur.com
> *This online magazine offers tons of great information on starting up your own business, working from home, and running your own auto franchise; it also lists educational and training opportunities.*

Specialty Equipment Market Association (SEMA)
P.O. Box 4910
Diamond Bar, CA 91765
www.sema.org
> *Members make, buy, sell, and use specialty parts and accessories to make vehicles more attractive, faster, safer, more fun, and even like new again. This organization holds a trade show every year in Las Vegas.*

CHAPTER NINE

Auto Club Jobs

We want to say up front that most auto enthusiast club tasks are voluntary. Even when clubs are for profit, they are almost invariably part-time activities. Still, the experience gained in club involvement can lead to employment in a range of other car-related careers.

In many clubs, people serve as unpaid officers. The Porsche Club of America (PCA), for example, lists these volunteer staff positions: president, vice president, secretary, treasurer, past president, and executive secretary. The PCA also lists these committees and special appointments:

- Awards, club racing (with five subcommittees)
- Finance
- Historian
- Insurance
- Legal advisor
- Legislative liaison
- Membership
- Newsletter
- Petition
- Parade (show)
- Parade advisory (with five subcommittees)
- Policy
- Procedures
- Public relations, safety
- Publications editor
- Region focus editor
- Special interest groups coordinator

- Technical (with ten subcommittees)
- Valuation

In short, there's something for everyone to do in an auto club, and there's an auto club for every type of auto enthusiast. Doing an online search using the keywords *auto club* will yield an impressive number of clubs for those interested in new or old cars—specific years or makes of cars.

....

Club Operator

The prerequisites for operating a single-make or one-marquee car club as a business are relatively simple, but the job may not be very profitable. Most club people must be devoted to and knowledgeable about one make of car and have numerous talents. They may need to keep ever-expanding files and engage in mail, fax, E-mail, and phone correspondence with owners of that make. They should be adept writers, since a member newsletter is the glue that keeps most clubs together. A computer background is also needed; it eases tedious record keeping and is the key to desktop newsletter publishing. Of course, having an E-mail address as a means for correspondence is necessary for most aspects of society today.

"A car club is fairly easy to run," according to Patrick Murphy of Spencer, Massachusetts. "You have to publish as good a newsletter as you can afford, set your dues within reason, and promote. The big thing is to be accessible to your members and perform a service for them.

"When I was living in New Hampshire, I founded a regional Oakland-Pontiac club. I advertised the club in *Hemmings* and signed up seventy members the first year. I made it very clear in the newsletter that I was running the club for profit, and that I depended on members' input; our job was to give them the services they wanted. They used the newsletter as a clearinghouse for parts and services wanted, cars wanted and for sale—all the usual needs."

Another important factor for having a successful car club is to hold a convention or meet that the members can attend to meet other enthusiasts. According to Murphy, some members made a five-hour trip to the Pontiac convention, and it was a great success.

While it isn't very profitable, it is possible to operate a car club as a money-making business. As long as you provide people with services of value for their money, they'll pay the dues and meet the fees to cover your costs and add a little profit.

When you first start your club, be careful not to overcommit yourself. If you plan to stage an event, figure out how many members you need to attend in order to break even, and ask for a show of interest before you actually schedule it. That way, when you do send out the news of the event, you should get enough paying guests to make it work.

The authors' experience as newsletter editor and director of the Delaware Valley Region of the Classic Car Club of America (CCCA) mirrors Patrick Murphy's, although ours was a nonprofit organization working to break even. We held our own local meets; staged meets in cooperation with other CCCA regions as well as other car clubs; and put on rallies, dinners, picnics, and tours to places as diverse as area museums, steam railways, and muzzle-loaders' festivals.

In addition, we frequently solicited member input on all our activities. Our newsletter reported events, ran members' ads, and earned some money from business advertisers. Unlike the Porsche Club of America and some others, our CCCA region did not automatically enroll all national members living in our area; we had to go after them just as we would have if we had operated a separate club.

Motorsports or Theme Park Operator

Bob Russo and Dick Muller Jr. are anything but strangers to auto enthusiasm in general and motorsports in particular. They met through their shared membership in the Porsche Club of

America. Russo was chief driving instructor for the local club region at the time, and Muller was his student.

The idea for a motorsports theme park was Muller's, but it was Bob Russo who had the years of racing and driving experience needed to mastermind the park's birth. It all started when the pair located four hundred acres near the Morgantown exit of the Pennsylvania Turnpike, close to Philadelphia, Allentown, Reading, Lancaster, Hershey, and Carlisle—in short, convenient for the area's many auto enthusiasts.

The first phase was a fifteen-acre autocross. Today, Formula Motorsports Park is the first country club for auto enthusiasts. The usual country club activities—golf, tennis, swimming, basketball, and a clubhouse with fine dining for up to four hundred—are augmented by a movie theater, an auto museum, libraries, and meeting rooms. In addition to the autocross course where drivers pilot their own cars, there is a three-mile road course and a go-cart track. By starting with an undeveloped location, the organizers were able to create a full-amenities club planned especially for driving enthusiasts, not a racetrack recycled for afternoon driving by sports car clubs and their amateur racers.

Even before the park opened, Muller and Russo had sold the 750 charter memberships. They had also enrolled twenty-five car clubs throughout the East, representing twenty-two thousand members. Among the proposed activities at the park are those in which enthusiasts with physical disabilities can participate.

Bob Russo has the automotive and marketing skills needed to make such a massive venture work, with more than thirty years of amateur and professional experience. In addition to being a Porsche Club of America member and skilled amateur high-performance driver, he worked for eleven years for the late Bob Holbert and the Holbert Racing Team. He coordinated the team's racing efforts at the Twenty-Four Hours of Daytona and at the Sebring, Florida, races. He was also general manager of Holbert

Racing Aftermarket Sales, which sold Porsche parts, accessories, and safety equipment.

In addition to the usual round of country club jobs, the theme park employs museum staff and public relations and publicity experts, plus driving instructors and track personnel to augment the volunteer timers, flag people, and communications staff that car clubs bring with them to help with members' motorsports participation.

It's a massive venture to undertake and to be successful, you need the business and marketing acumen to attract financial backers and publicize the business in order to secure memberships. If successful, however, you may have a very profitable business.

Additional Resources

In addition to many of the unique and varied clubs mentioned in this chapter, the following organizations may prove interesting to you as well as a good source of information for further career exploration. Keep in mind that there's probably a club available for any area of interest, and a quick online search using keywords such as *car* or *automobile* and *club*—or even specific makes and models—may yield additional resources.

Antique Automobile Club of America (AACA)
501 West Governor Road
P.O. Box 417
Hershey, PA 17033
www.aaca.org

> *This large club features an extensive website that offers information on forums, meets, and local chapters, as well as instructional videos, films, and merchandise. It also provides links to a variety of other automotive clubs.*

United States Auto Club
USAC National Office
4910 West Sixteenth Street
Speedway, IN 46224
www.usacracing.com

> *The United States Auto Club provides information about sanctioned events, the latest news in the sport, and track directories.*

CHAPTER TEN

Jobs with Kits and Models

These careers are grouped together because the people who pursue them often have characteristics in common. Whether the job is designing or marketing car models, model kits, full-size kit cars, or factory-built replicas, the uniting thread is a degree of respect for the original car.

Some modern full-size replicas of older cars, called "replicars," are less than faithful to the originals. Other so-called replicars ape the styling of a period car without duplicating a specific model. Most are not perfect duplicates, ignoring the correct instruments and other details, for instance. But nearly all kit cars and factory replicars have to compromise in such matters as drivetrains and power plants. They're low-volume cars, so duplicating an original engine, gearbox, or instrument cluster would be outrageously expensive. Its modern engine and drivetrain often make a kit car or replicar a better bet for the highway than its namesake.

Economy is another reason for buying a scale model or a full-size replicar. With original Shelby Cobras costing several hundred thousand dollars, even a $45,000 Cobra look-alike is a relative bargain. And at anything from $9 to $1,000, scale models are a relatively economical way to indulge a taste for exotic cars.

The parallel of buying ready-made or in form is common to scale models and replicars. Scale models come complete or as kits to assemble. (One company occasionally advertises its willingness to pay a hobbyist $1,000 to assemble all 2,368 parts of the Pocher 1:8-scale Mercedes 540K for resale to a collector or hobby shop.) With tools, garage space, and patience, it is possible to turn a lowly

VW frame, suspension, and wheels into a full-size Porsche Speed-ster look-alike or a rear-engine MG-TD. The work is as hard as restoring, but the results may be worth the effort as you will cer-tainly pay more for a factory-built replicar. Even at several thou-sand dollars, it costs only a fraction of what the real thing would sell for—if you could find one.

Either way, the kit car owner isn't afraid to drive this new cre-ation, but some people in the car hobby have low opinions of kit car or replicar safety. Few factory makers last long enough to produce great numbers of kits, but there are resources for those interested.

Glenn Pray of Tulsa, Oklahoma, produced a very successful seven-eighths-size Cord 812, and Beck Development of Upland, California, turns out a much-sought-after Porsche 550 Spider replicar. Crown Publishing publishes a kit car buyer's guide and a monthly magazine, *Kit Car Marketer & Cobra Trader*. Petersen Publishing offers *Kit Car*, a bimonthly magazine on the same sub-ject, and McMullen & Yee Publishing's bimonthly is named *Kit Car Illustrated*.

....

Model Design, Manufacturing, and Marketing

The Franklin Mint is the world's leading creator and direct mar-keter of heirloom-quality collectibles. With a customer base of more than eight million collectors and sixty gallery retail stores, it's listed as the twenty-seventh-most-advertised brand in Amer-ica, and has more than forty-five hundred employees worldwide (more than sixteen hundred at its Pennsylvania headquarters alone). Creating detailed yet affordable car models in scales from 1:43 to 1:6 calls for the services of a great many skilled people. The design and replication quality of the 129 auto, truck, and motor-cycle models currently offered for sale are the ultimate responsi-bility of professionally trained designers.

A design team works together following the input of the marketing staff and customers on what models to build and in which scale. Once a choice is made, researchers have to find actual examples of the car and secure the manufacturer's authorization or licensing agreement to reproduce the car in miniature. When possible, Franklin Mint copies factory drawings and other original documents. The team also studies an example car and photographs it completely—every detail. Once Franklin Mint designers have all the information, from original paint color to correct tire tread pattern, the real work begins.

"Using all the input at hand, we make many basic decisions," explains design manager Raffi Minasian. "Does one color scheme have historic significance for this particular model? Should the steering wheel and front wheels turn? Should doors, hoods, and trunks open? Should we incorporate 'squish' into the model's seats? We try to take as few liberties with the real thing as possible because many of our model collectors know the real thing."

Draftspeople then prepare hand-drawn or computer-generated plans of the model, usually to twice the scale. Then, just like the real car makers, they produce a "buck"—a hand-built version of the car. "Theirs are life-size; ours are twice scale," says Minasian. Once refined, they produce actual size plans from which die makers can make the stamping dies used for the metal parts and the casting dies used for the plastic items. Every one of these jobs calls for exceptional levels of craftsmanship. By the time the cars are finished, it has cost the scale equivalent of what it cost the manufacturer to design and build the original.

The late Gordon Buehrig, designer of classic Auburns and the 812 Cord and the first design manager of diecast models for the Franklin Mint, once said, "No one in his right mind would go through all this to make a model car."

From his dedication, it is apparent that Raffi Minasian does not agree. Minasian came to his job through a combination of factors, not the least of which is respect for the automobile bordering on awe. He acquired his art and design background at UCLA and later attended the Art Center in Pasadena, where he emerged at the top of the class.

He began his career as a full-time designer for major manufacturers, including car makers and toy companies (he worked on Hot Wheels, among other projects). He immersed himself in auto history and research and started marketing auto-related pieces of writing and illustrations for auto magazines. He also taught auto design part-time at the Art Institute of Seattle and industrial design at the University of Washington.

Minasian says of his current position as design manager for Franklin Mint Precision Models: "This job is, to me, the culmination of what I love and have been trained to do. It combines my love of automobiles with respect for their designs and designers. I'm actively involved with documentation, history, accuracy, and writing." It gives me an exceptional opportunity to acknowledge the existence of the single most significant icon of the twentieth century. Nothing else stimulates all a person's senses like the automobile. As you see a fine car, you can place yourself on a visual journey back in time, one that is not equaled anywhere else in our culture. That is what makes these rolling sculptures so exciting."

....

Model Maker

Pierre Decrouez of Swarthmore, Pennsylvania, plans, installs, and upgrades computer systems for businesses. But this multitalented man also designs and builds scale models from scratch. Past work includes a nine-foot-long destroyer complete in every detail, among several astonishing miniatures.

His latest project places him in the center of two fast-growing automotive subcultures: collecting old stationary engines and models and miniatures. Prices for real farm engines and old Maytag washing machine gas engines have risen to the point where Pierre can command a handsome figure for his one-sixth-scale working model of the New Holland stationary engine. This was the old "one-lunger," the half-horsepower one-cylinder stationary gas engine that powered farm equipment from 1908 until rural electrification killed it off in the 1930s.

Decrouez's interest in miniatures is so great that he not only wears a jeweler's loop (magnifying eyepiece) when making models, he carries one wherever he goes. He has created his New Holland model entirely from scratch. He made thirty-three castings for its machine parts and markets each engine assembled and ready to run. All moving parts are brass, except for a steel crankshaft, stainless steel cylinder walls, and aluminum pistons. Instead of the splash-feed lubrication of the original, Decrouez adds a few drops of oil to the gasoline he uses. This, and battery-fired ignition instead of a magneto, are his only departures from authenticity.

It's a thrill to see this little engine run. It fits comfortably in the palm of your hand, including its wood base. To start it, Decrouez inserts gas into a tiny reservoir from a metal squeeze can with a hypodermic spout. He spins one of the twin brass flywheels a few times, and it starts up. After an initial hesitation, it settles into the odd, loping rhythm of the original. Only the exhaust note emanating from the scale-size muffler differs from the real thing. It is a bit higher on the chromatic scale.

Pierre Decrouez markets his engine through appearances at vintage engine and model shows. Advertising is word-of-mouth. Clearly, that's all he needs. He has orders as of this writing for the first fifty working models, complete even to one-sixth-size patent plates containing one-sixth-size consecutive serial numbers. The price for these tiny engines run up to $1,200 each. Ironically, this is about one-sixth the price of a full-size New Holland—if you could find one in fine working order.

....

Model Marketer

Enter the tidy town of Berkeley Heights, New Jersey, find the EWA Automobilia Center in a ground-floor retail mall, and you step into a small new world. The majority of items are on four wheels and in 1.43 scale.

There's a synergy between models and full-size cars. Some people start with a car model—perhaps a kit they build—and go from there to the real thing. Or it can work the other way. People collect models of the cars their families never had (and that they wanted as youngsters) or of cars they wish they could afford today.

Eric Waiter saw a market for British auto enthusiast magazines in this country, and in 1982 started EWA as a basement business that processes sales and subscriptions for *Motorsport* and *Classic & Sports Car,* two popular British magazines. He added a few car model lines. EWA Automobilia Center continued as a basement business, combing model makers worldwide for new items and marketing entirely by mail. In 1988, Waiter opened a store. Over time, he and his staff expanded the EWA catalog, added more automobile magazine titles plus books and videos, and took on many more model lines.

"We are still 95 percent a mail-order business," Waiter says, "and I believe we are now the largest marketer of car models in the United States and possibly in the world." Waiter stocks up to nine thousand models in several scales, sells copies or processes subscriptions for twenty-eight British auto magazines, maintains an inventory of three thousand auto book titles, and stocks some six hundred auto videos and related items.

Computers now manage the entire EWA inventory, the catalog, and most of the marketing efforts. The company advertises in magazines in the United States, Europe, and Japan and ships worldwide. The latest EWA catalog is 120 pages jammed with every EWA model, book, video, poster, and piece of miscellany offered. EWA is also online at www.ewa1.com.

Browsing the EWA catalog or website is convenient, but there's nothing like being there and seeing case after case of tiny classics, racers old and new, trucks, buses, and collector cars of all kinds. It is truly the ultimate garage.

Additional Resources

The Franklin Mint
U.S. Route 1
Franklin Center, PA 19091
www.franklinmint.com

Kit Car
Crown Communications
26949 Whitehorse Place
Santa Clarita, CA 91387
www.kitcarmag.com
> *This magazine includes feature and technical articles, events, classifieds, and buyer's guides.*

Kitcarmagazine.com
> *This online magazine features a variety of useful information for kit car enthusiasts.*

CHAPTER ELEVEN

Working in a Library or Museum

It seems that the stereotype "Marian the Librarian" (from *The Music Man*) is about as out-of-date as a 1908 Ford Model T. Yesterday's librarians are today's information managers, as adept with computers and the Internet as they are with the Dewey decimal system. Not everyone in the field today has a degree in library science or information management, but such a degree is a virtual necessity for future careerists.

Varied opportunities exist for those who wish to combine automotive interest with some form of information management. One job possibility is with public libraries. Here, one librarian or library assistant amasses an automotive collection by grouping and cataloging all auto-related materials in one location for the convenience of users. A greater opportunity for combining cataloging talents and automotive knowledge is working as the auto book buyer for a bookstore chain. Some auto museums also have libraries and research facilities where information managers can find jobs. But the library may be just one place among many for a staff member of a smaller museum. Jobs as literature curators with auto museums or large private car collections also exist, although they usually encompass other duties not related to cars.

Librarian or Archivist

There are probably fewer than a dozen people in this country who manage large automotive library collections. There are three vast auto literature collections at the public libraries in Detroit and

Lansing, Michigan, and in Los Angeles, and the headquarters of the Antique Automobile Club of America in Hershey, Pennsylvania, has a major collection. Another possibility for auto-minded historians, librarians, and researchers is to be an archivist for an automobile manufacturer (the Ford Motor Company Archives in Dearborn, Michigan, is an excellent example).

The Free Library of Philadelphia's automotive collection dates from 1948, when Thomas McKean, an avid auto enthusiast, donated a trove of early automotive literature with the provision that he serve as its curator. Unfortunately, McKean died in an auto accident shortly afterward. In a 1953 reorganization, the library combined McKean's gift with other auto-related materials in one reference area. Later donations included a substantial collection from the Society of Automotive Historians. The library continues to add to its auto-related holdings, but all the items are on reserve for the use of researchers and cannot be checked out. Today, the collection includes approximately:

- 32,000 photographs
- 31,000 items of sales literature
- 14,000 magazines
- 7,300 instruction books
- 6,000 books
- 3,000 35 mm slides
- 2,400 shop manuals

Lou Helverson is a career librarian. He began working at the Free Library of Philadelphia in 1952 while still in high school. He taught for two years (he holds a B.S. in elementary education from Temple University), and then he returned to the library and earned a master's degree in library science from Drexel University. He served as a branch librarian for twelve years and took over the automotive collection.

Helverson combines no-nonsense pragmatism and natural good humor with a researcher's curiosity, vast subject knowledge, and infinite patience. All these attributes are needed to cope with a boggling array of auto-related questions and problems. In a typical month, he and one assistant gave out 230 auto prices by phone, replied to letters requesting data or photos from eight states and five foreign countries, and answered requests ranging from the easy (1967 Jaguar wiring diagram) and difficult (everything about the Keeley Motor) to the near-impossible (a query on a 1900 Reber from a Canadian museum).

Challenges can range from decoding vehicle identification numbers (VINs) to creating a bibliography on social issues and the automobile during the 1920s. Helverson may have to unearth everything known about the Witt Engine Works one day and research Ford Pinto gas tank explosion litigation the next. He gets calls from lawyers seeking car values for divorce or estate settlements and from forensic investigators needing crash data on specific cars. Naturally, he gets calls from collectors pursuing every imaginable subject and from do-it-yourselfers needing repair information on recent models.

Two other curatorial responsibilities are acquisitions and cataloging. Helverson has standing orders for each year's new auto repair manuals and magazine subscriptions and also gets notices of just about all the new auto books published. "It's my job to choose those that will be best for the collection while fitting into the library's budget," he says. Helverson tries to let his own personality influence the collection. "I have to do this based on what we need, not what I like."

Cataloging is "a problem-filled area," according to Helverson. "We use the Dewey decimal system as far as it will go, but for photographs and a lot of the literature, we have to catalog by vehicle make, model, and year." Now the library is beginning to acquire videotapes and DVDs, which are a new cataloging obstacle to sort out. "We have a lot of the collection on microfilm, including shop manuals through 1985, but the whole data thing is getting harder to manage. More manufacturers and auto service companies are supplying information on CD-ROM. And no two automotive resources—manufacturers or other libraries—catalog their data the same way. There are no universal descriptions. What one library may call 'auto literature,' another will catalog as 'marketing brochures.'" Because there is currently no standard, it is very hard for researchers to exchange computerized information.

Despite the frustrations of trying to help callers who think the curators are over-the-phone auto mechanics or who lack the knowledge to pose answerable questions, the job has its rewards. "It's really great when I can send the guy restoring a rare car some pictures or facts he couldn't get anywhere else. It's worth the whole day's work."

....

Museum Curator or Director

The Directory of American Automotive Museums and Displays, published by Eagle One Industries, lists 130 auto museums and public displays in the United States and Canada. There is a museum for Jaguars, one for Stanley Steamers, and another for Harley-Davidson motorcycles. Other especially interesting museums include Cole Palen's Old Rhinebeck Aerodrome in New York, where actors fly vintage aircraft and drive old cars in outdoor shows on summer weekends; the Auburn-Cord-Duesenberg Museum, the only museum where the cars are displayed where they were built; and Heritage Plantation of Sandwich, Massachusetts, with its viewer-friendly collection of landmark vehicles housed in a replica of a Shaker round stone barn. California has more automotive museums than any other state, with fourteen in all.

Whether you're the curator of the recently opened National Corvette Museum in the car's hometown of Bowling Green, Kentucky, or the director of a varied museum such as Los Angeles' Petersen Museum, the requirements are much the same: intense knowledge of one car make or of many makes—and in one or more periods of automotive history—plus the ability to direct or even perform a panorama of management and personnel jobs.

Deane Fehrman trained to be a teacher and taught for a time after becoming certified. But for ten years before undertaking his present career—automotive appraiser and appraisal class teacher—he was curator of the Veteran Car Museum in Denver, Colorado.

He applied for the curator's job and was accepted on the spot, he recalls, "because I brought a wealth of personal knowledge and experience in the collection and preservation of automotive literature and memorabilia from my own collection." His collecting passion, dating from childhood, continues to this day. Although just a few years out of college at the time, Deane Fehrman was wise enough in automotive ways to land the job and direct the museum for a decade.

The Veteran Car Museum was the culmination of one collector's dream. The museum's founder, the late Arthur G. Rippey Jr., was well versed in automotive lore from his years as a Detroit advertising executive. During the 1930s as he worked in Detroit, he developed a great respect for and knowledge of the cars of this period. He moved to Denver to open what became the largest advertising agency in the Rocky Mountain area.

Once in Denver, Rippey struck gold—what Fehrman calls magnificent vintage cars languishing in the garages of those who had made their fortunes in the mines of Colorado—when he bought a pair of Rolls-Royce Silver Ghosts for $350 and started the collection that became the Veteran Car Museum.

"We shared the idea of wanting to give deserving cars a good home, and Mr. Rippey had made quite a start when I arrived," Fehrman says. During his years as curator, Fehrman helped Rippey find and purchase cars to create a select if not huge collection. At various times, the collection numbered from twenty-five to thirty-five vehicles. Among them were a 1941 Cadillac once owned by Mamie Eisenhower, two Duesenbergs, one of the two Silver Ghosts, long-wheelbase Pike's Peak tour buses and "climbers," and several other local-interest vehicles.

"I've had the pleasure of being able to drive everything the museum had without the pain of ownership," Fehrman says. "I have no jealousy over not owning these cars."

Being a museum curator is hard work that calls many talents into play. A curator is the custodian of all museum materials and exhibits. He or she develops, refines, and maintains the museum's focus. A curator must be adept at cataloguing and filing every item in the collection and be responsible for accessions (buying vehicles and parts) and deaccessions (selling what is no longer wanted). These duties demand expert knowledge of car prices and values.

Unlike some curators who are concerned only with their museums' collections, Deane Fehrman also performed a host of other museum jobs that are often carried out by separate department heads in larger museums and often considered independent careers. He was the de facto public relations director, responsible for dealing with the visiting public and promoting the exhibits. His discerning eye for vehicle correctness, developed through car trading during his college years, made him the logical choice to supervise restorations and to hire qualified mechanics to improve and maintain the collection. But the job that helped qualify him for his later career—specialty vehicle appraiser—was the extensive research needed to ensure the authenticity and historical accuracy of every step in the mechanical or aesthetic restoration of every museum vehicle.

"Museum curating led me to the broader field of appraising. A continuous thirst for automotive knowledge is what you must have to perform either job well," he adds.

Larger museums can have separate curators for vehicles, literature, and artifacts or memorabilia. Other museum careers not previously mentioned, along with a capsule summary of needed skills, include:

- Admissions clerks, gift shop personnel, general helpers—little or no automotive experience required.
- Business manager—accounting and administration skills.
- Docent or exhibit guide—specific automotive and exhibits knowledge (often in conjunction with research duties).
- Exhibits planner or designer—art or aesthetic background with design and construction experience.
- Upholsterers, painters, woodworkers, and other vehicle restoration specialists—related job experience (larger museums only).

....

Auto-Related Memorabilia Marketer

People who like cars—especially old cars—often collect auto-related memorabilia. One example of related memorabilia is early filling station and garage equipment, gas pumps, product containers, and advertising signs. Auto literature is another. Kits and models are a third. There are many more collectibles, from kids' pedal cars to hood ornaments, old auto magazines and books to advertising paraphernalia. Many automaniacs also collect unrelated items, which includes anything mechanical that appeared in the last century, the Auto Era. These collectibles include vintage aircraft, player pianos and player rolls, wooden boats, early outboard motors, vending machines and juke boxes, old firearms, calliopes, and so on.

Along with a home-based parts-locating business and car club operation, Patrick Murphy buys and sells automotive memorabilia. His passion is models of sixties muscle cars, and to build his collection, he trades just about anything else he can find.

Whether he is scouting toy and model magazines or snooping around flea markets and auto swap meets, Murphy is always on the lookout for something auto-related that he either wants to keep or that is priced low enough so he can buy it and resell it at a profit. "It doesn't matter whether it's early car magazines, toys, parts and accessories, ads and manufacturers' literature, whatever," Murphy explains. "I'm on the alert for bargains. I am selective. If I don't want to keep it, or don't think I can sell it quickly, I don't buy it."

As with his parts resale business, Murphy keeps alert to price changes almost day to day. These changes are judged as much by instinct and swap-meet bargaining as by any formal means. "You develop knowledge over the years" for which items are worth what amount, according to Murphy.

"I'm not a real specialist, like someone who markets nothing but old car ads or service manuals. I like it all, and I know a little bit about all of it."

One of Murphy's ambitions is to start a booth for auto-related items at a regular antiques flea market. He says that some dealers have an occasional tin toy car or scale model, but he's never seen one stand that sold nothing but old car memorabilia. "I think there's enough interest among general antique fanciers for an auto-items-only vendor," Murphy adds. "I'd like to try that."

Many people who deal with memorabilia are also finding success by marketing their second-hand treasures on the Internet by posting them with online auctions or with the dealers' personal websites. This allows for a reach outside of the local flea market or a particular region of the country.

······························

Additional Resources

National Automobile Museum
10 Lake Street South
Reno, NV 89501
www.automuseum.org
> *This interesting website offers a range of information, including research services for automotive restorers, scholars, journalists, enthusiasts, and the interested public.*

Detroit Public Library
National Automotive History Collection (NAHC)
5201 Woodward Avenue
Detroit, MI 48202
www.detroit.lib.mi.us/nahc

The NAHC is perhaps the most well-respected automotive history collection in the country. The NAHC documents the history and development of the automobile and contains resources of more than six hundred thousand processed items, including thousands of photographs depicting the automobile's historical, social, mechanical, and design aspects that are available for public viewing, research, and publication.

CHAPTER TWELVE

Jobs for Number Crunchers

ome number-crunching jobs require the ability to establish the value of a car, truck, or motor home. These jobs include adjuster, appraiser, and insurer. The auto knowledge needed can range from current body shop hourly rates and repair parts costs to the values of a once-restored classic or of a hoary antique just rescued from someone's barn. The degrees of automotive knowledge needed vary with the specific job.

Adjuster

Most adjusters work for auto insurance companies, determining the extent and cost of accident damage and deciding what's to be done with the car or truck. Whether they choose to scrap the vehicle or have it repaired depends on the extent of the damage, the repair costs, and the vehicle's preaccident value. If the repairs would cost more than the car is worth, the owner receives the current value in cash to buy a replacement. Otherwise, the insurance company pays to have the car repaired, based on a body shop's estimate. Large insurance companies employ adjusters, but this can also be a freelance career. Many adjusters work for several companies and are paid according to the claims they settle.

Mike Karli is an auto claims adjuster employed by a major national insurer. As an adjuster working in Pennsylvania, he is licensed and has had to pass a proficiency test. Unlike many adjusters, Mike also wears an appraiser's hat, and his official job title is claim representative. As such, he deals with the public as well as with repair shops, and his job performance is measured by his customer service skills as well as appraisal and claims settlement abilities. Since he settles about fifty claims a month, or more than six hundred a year at an average cost to the company of $1,500, he is responsible for dispensing nearly a million dollars of the company's money each year.

Years ago, claimants obtained two or three estimates from different body shops for repairs, which led to body shops lowballing their estimates to get the work, which often led to problems. Now most insurance companies deal with whatever shop the customer chooses.

As Mike explains, "Insurance companies set the hourly labor rates, and shops usually accept this. There are times when they want more, and I have to deal with that case by case. Negotiating with the body shop is one aspect of the job. I also try to make each customer as happy as I can. It's not easy because almost every person believes his or her car is worth more than the appraisal."

Mike's firm uses computer software to arrive at a car's preaccident value, help with the estimating, and display the costs for new or aftermarket parts. These programs have made the appraisal process significantly faster and more streamlined. "I can do an appraisal of any car made in recent years in less than five minutes. I can get parts costs, too. When I check these dollar figures with the shop's repair estimate, I can make a repair-or-scrap decision on the spot," Mike says. "That's 85 percent of the work. The rest depends on my judgment, which includes assessing the preaccident condition of the car. If there was body damage before the accident, I have to down value the car to cover it."

Will the company get an expert opinion in an unusual case? "Yes, although they try to have us do the difficult settlements, too. I recently settled the claim for a man restoring an early Mustang at home. The house and garage burned, destroying the car, his records, and a lot of parts he claimed to have bought for the restoration. I settled for an average of prices for restored Mustangs in *Hemmings Motor News*."

Salaried claims adjusters can earn in the mid $20,000 range a year to start. Salaries rise to near $60,000 after twenty-five to thirty years, and recent statistics show that the median annual earnings income is $41,080. Mike says that the field is still open to anyone with a college degree who can pass a proficiency exam after several weeks of training. About one-third of the states require independent, or public, adjusters to be licensed, but the requirements vary by state. Claims adjusters working for companies can usually work under the company license and do not need to become licensed.

Basic computer skills are a job necessity, and many adjusters are now equipped with laptop computers so they can have instant access to the necessary forms and files they need. Past automotive experience is not needed, and only about 20 percent of adjusters come from the auto repair industry. Local or regional travel is usually required, and since most information can be retrieved from a laptop, many adjusters work from their homes.

For additional information, go to the Independent Automotive Damage Appraiser Association website at www.iada.org.

· · · · · · · · · · · · · · · · · · · ·

Appraiser

The old joke has it that a car buff saw a newspaper ad: "1957 Mercedes 300SL gullwing, perfect, $5,000" with a phone number. He called the number, got a woman who confirmed the ad's correctness, rushed right out with cash, and bought the car. Before he drove away, the thrilled new owner said to the woman, "Why did you do that? It's worth $250,000!" She answered, "My husband ran off with his secretary and wired me, 'Sell the Mercedes and send me the money.'" Obviously, the husband's mind was on anything but seeing an auto appraiser before he departed.

In *The Floating Opera*, John Barth wrote, "Nothing is intrinsically valuable; the value of everything is attributed to it . . . by people." The expert auto appraiser is called upon to estimate the value of a vintage, exotic, or unusual car for which there is no easy answer (for example, the NADA Used Car Guide may no longer list its value). The appraiser may have to set a special value to settle an accident insurance repair claim that is beyond an everyday adjuster's experience, to assist in divorce or estate settlements, to set an auction reserve figure, to determine replacement value for a new insurance policy or collateral for loans, to assist a business dissolution, or to fix a federal tax deduction amount when an old car is donated to charity. An appraiser may also be hired by a prospective purchaser for an independent value to compare to the seller's price. Qualified appraisers also serve as expert witnesses when matters of automotive value land in court.

An appraiser works for a fixed fee plus expenses. The fee is not related to the value of the car being appraised; if it were so based, this would constitute a conflict of interest.

Deane Fehrman pursued his teaching career for many years before he turned his avocation of collecting mechanical antiques and auto-related memorabilia into a vocation by becoming an auto museum manager and curator (see Chapter 11). Now one of the country's best-known antique auto appraisers and arbiters, he is chairman of the Automotive Specialties Group of the American Society of Appraisers. He is also on the market advisory panel of *Collector Car & Truck Prices* magazine and operates his own organization, Antique Automobile Appraisals, in Golden, Colorado. The firm appraises horseless carriages, sports cars, special-interest autos, kit cars, fire apparatus, classic and milestone autos, trucks, race cars, and even vintage trolleys.

This resume-like summary gives no clue to Deane Fehrman's thoughtful approach to appraisals. That arises from his lifelong fascination with collecting.

His love of full-size cars started as a young boy. "My father worked part-time perfecting an automobile cigarette lighter. I remember that his partner would drive to our house in a yellow 1948 Packard custom convertible. I used to stare, fascinated, at that gleaming cormorant hood ornament. It, among other things, fueled my collecting fever. I have that chrome-plated ornament today."

Fehrman paid some of his college expenses by buying and reselling rust-free Arizona cars, an experience that helped form his opinions and build his store of knowledge. "I favor well-maintained original cars over restored ones. A restoration is only as good as the least well-done part. Top-quality painting can be undercut by sloppy or unauthentic stitching on a restored interior. An unrestored car has an inherent correctness, a mellowness. If it's been well kept, the paint looks right. The leather smells right. Even the mildew is correct!"

An appraiser must look at a given car with total objectivity. For example, his or her job may be to estimate the fair market value as part of a divorce settlement. Fair market value is defined as the price a willing and knowledgeable buyer would pay a willing and knowledgeable seller. Like a good test driver, an appraiser must experience an auto in order to know how it should handle, appear, and compare mechanically with others of its kind that he or she has recently appraised. Condition is the most important consideration of value. This requires a detailed physical inspection. Authenticity and originality, both crucial to value, must be judged by someone who is an expert in certain cars, but expertise is a process of accumulating knowledge. Fehrman is still learning about cars—even after ten years as a museum curator and sixteen years as a full-time appraiser.

Fehrman asserts that appraisals are as much an art as a science. There is more than one "value" for a particular auto. In fact, this lack of a firm value is what changed his career. "Before it became fashionable to own an old car, people would come to the museum and ask for car appraisals for divorces, insurance settlements, and such. I realized that I (and the museum) could be held legally liable for any appraisal answers that backfired. Asking me 'What's my 1932 K Lincoln worth?' was as full of potential legal problems as asking a doctor you meet at a party to diagnose your sore back.

So I contacted the American Society of Appraisers and enrolled in its appraisal theory courses over the years. With that completed, and with the required experience, I became an ASA member and made appraisal my career."

Appraisals are either preventive (before a loss) or remedial (afterward). The intended use of an appraisal is as important in estimating automotive value as the desirability, condition, and authenticity of the vehicle. With the following story, Fehrman illustrates how one car can have several values, depending on the context in which it is appraised.

"I was asked years ago to appraise a restored MG-TD. My client had won the car in a soft drink company's contest. The public relations company that staged the contest had sold the car to the soft drink people for $19,000, and this was the value stated by them in the contest. But the winner was not happy because he had to pay taxes on the car's value. Only when I saw him did I understand why this car was no prize. He was seventy-eight years old and six-feet-eight-inches tall. He couldn't even get into the car, and so, of course, he didn't want it. I appraised it for tax purposes at $13,000 (the restoration wasn't all that good). But since the owner wanted out, he sold the car for $9,000. So, in different contexts, that car had three different but equally 'true' values."

A college degree in valuation science or related appraisal and automotive experience, ASA membership, and continuing education at seminars and workshops are decided career assets. To be a regular ASA member requires passing association courses and working as an appraiser for two years; senior membership requires five years of active appraisal work. The appraisal profession's demands are many. The work involves continuing education, travel, reaccreditation, conferences, seminars, pretrial conferences, court trials, cross-examinations, photography, retainer fees, recertification, auctions, files, forms, faxes, phones, and networking.

Although Deane Fehrman still collects for himself, he now has a new hobby since his old one has become his vocation. His latest toy, devoid of "value contexts" and all other complications, is a four-by-four tractor that lets him plow snow, cut wood, and do other fun things.

....

Insurer

Most auto insurance companies market through insurance agents who sell every type of coverage and usually aren't car buffs. Someone in the insurance company head office will price out your policy by combining risk tables based on where you live with valuation tables showing what your car is worth and evaluating the coverage you want. But the rare car needs more than commodity insurance. This is where the insurance companies that advertise in *Hemmings Motor News* and other automotive publications enter the picture. They insure the vehicles that are out of the mainstream and usually at considerable savings over conventional insurance companies based on limited car use and garage storage. Regular insurers are not prepared for unusual vehicles, and generally they shy away from coverage.

Gerry Charvat of Leo, Indiana, and his wife, Sandy, are in the specialty car insurance business. They came to it by way of their street rod business, which they started after they decided to leave corporate jobs to pursue other more personal and satisfying interests. They turned their street rod hobby into a good business. They grew into the insurance segment through one of their rod customers who was the senior vice president of an insurance company that wanted to pursue the hot rod or street rod market.

The company sent Sandy to school. She studied for her Indiana insurance license and passed the state exam. (Indiana also requires license holders to take fifteen hours of continuing education a year; states vary in their requirements.) When she earned her license, she was put in charge of insuring classic and special-interest cars.

When Sandy left that company, she and Gerry thought about their options. "We weren't set up to operate an agency," Gerry recalls, "but we liked the insurance business and started looking for an insurance carrier we could represent. We were contacted by one we really liked and who liked the proposal we wrote for street rod insurance, which was new to the company. After a lot of confusion, the bottom line was this: the carrier agreed to let us start our own agency to sell insurance. We became the exclusive agent nationally for street rods, and now we insure any special-interest vehicle.

"Now, as Collector Car Insurance, we have become licensed in forty-two states. Each state has different licensing requirements, and it would cost someone wanting to do the same thing about $15,000 to become licensed nationwide.

"Being able to establish car values for insurance purposes has its problems, but Sandy is as much a part of my car businesses as I am, and she has a lot of built-in knowledge, especially about street rod values, which are very hard to determine. Some of the 'name' rod shops, especially in California, really overprice the rods they build. It takes a rod builder—or his wife—to know that.

"We have to dig for our numbers, especially for street rods. There are no valuation guides on them. Street rod valuation is very difficult at best because each vehicle is made to the owner's likes and wants. Being avid street rodders for years and having built several cars for ourselves, we understand the blood, sweat, and tears that go into a project, along with the costs involved."

To value specialty cars, you need to study valuation books and research serial numbers to determine the value of comparable cars. All this digging and attention to detail is what makes a specialty car insurer different from the people with computer-generated valuations. This involves a more thoughtful and studious approach to assigning value to a car—especially if there's nothing quite like it to reference for comparison.

Automotive Analyst

Another numeric field is automotive analyst. These are the people who calculate and forecast automotive trends. Most work in the investment industry and are not necessarily auto enthusiasts. Foretelling the automotive future is not all that different from other types of industrial forecasting. An automotive analyst is simply an investment analyst who specializes in the automotive sector. In fact, the job is not about cars; it is about investing. While you need solid training in investment and forecasting in order to obtain and excel in the job, this is one number-crunching job that lets car buffs get paid for keeping up-to-the-minute on all the new developments and future trends of the industry they love.

Additional Resources

For more information on training and education in the fields of specialty appraisal, contact the following organizations:

American Society of Appraisers
555 Herndon Parkway, Suite 125
Herndon, VA 20170
www.appraisers.org

Appraisers Association of America
386 Park Avenue South, Suite 2000
New York, NY 10016
www.appraisersassoc.org

International Claim Association
1255 Twenty-Third Street NW
Washington, DC 20037
www.claim.org

Independent Automotive Damage Appraisers
   Association
P.O. Box 1166
Nixa, MO 65714
www.iada.org

National Association of Public Insurance Adjusters
112-J Eldon Street
Herndon, VA 20170
www.napia.com

Registered Professional Adjusters, Inc.
P.O. Box 3239
Napa, CA 94558
www.rpa-adjuster.com

CHAPTER THIRTEEN

Jobs with Art and Autos

From its earliest days, the automobile has attracted artists and sculptors. Edward Penfield and J. C. Leyendecker imparted their distinctive illustrative styles to 1907 and 1909 Pierce-Arrow advertisements, and they were far from the first to do so. The late Peter Helck devoted a long artistic career almost entirely to automotive oil paintings, sketches, and sculptures in a style that combined drama and realism. His cars were shown in motion, much as they appear in early racing photographs. Other fine artists and poster designers illustrated early auto races in the United States and in Europe. The stars of today include Ken Dallison (collage-style watercolors), Dale Klee (abandoned old car scenes), and Dennis Simon (posters, neckwear, and other media).

Other practitioners of automotive artistry include the combination engineer-illustrator, such as David Kimble, who specializes in auto cutaways; people who do art work for collector plates; and those who design new cars (see Chapter 2) and hot rods (Chapter 3). Then there are people who combine artistic ability or sensibility with a love of automobiles in the role of auto magazine art director or automotive book designer. The common career ingredients: a basic art talent, formal art training, and career determination. Today, computer graphics is also an essential skill.

Another variation is the artist who uses the car itself as a canvas. A few of these are famous artists apart from their automotive work. David Hockney's abstract painting for BMW, executed directly on an 850 CSi, is a good example and one in a series BMW is collecting.

Another artist now concerned with autos is Hiro Yamagata. This graduate of the Ecole des Beaux-Arts in Paris uses varied styles and media to avoid having his work categorized. A favorite among collectors for his scenes of cities he loves, Yamagata has embarked on a second body of work—twenty-four bodies, in fact. He is having twenty-four Mercedes-Benz 220A cabriolets restored, on which he will create an entire art exhibit titled "Earthly Paradise." The restored cars are left in white primer, then totally painted by Yamagata and his students in floral patterns the artist has sketched.

The first six cars have been shown in Los Angeles; it will take some time to complete the group. Eventually, the cars will probably be sold. *Automobile* magazine wrote of this epic effort: "Unlike a Yamagata on your wall that requires an invitation and action on the part of your friends to come over and see it, a piece from the 'Earthly Paradise' collection could simply be driven over to their house and shared."

Artist or Illustrator

Dennis Simon of Sparks, Maryland, wanted to combine his two collecting hobbies—antique cars and antique auto racing posters—and turn them into a business related to his art. Although his talent was recognized early, it took a great deal of work for Simon to earn the high place he now enjoys in automotive art circles.

After he graduated from art school, Simon spent a period of time doing freelance art for advertising agencies and United States government publications. One plum assignment stretched into a thirteen-year stint designing park exhibit systems for the National Park Service. Eventually, Simon had had enough of more conventional art assignments. He began developing an art style that echoed his interest in vintage racing cars. Not quite "vintage," as defined by antique car clubs, these cars—mostly European—were designed and built or modified for road and/or track racing and date from about 1920 to 1970.

He immersed himself in the racing scene and painted sample ideas for vintage-style racing posters. He marketed several of these to vintage auto racing clubs. Success came quickly through a combination of natural artistic ability, his style (reminiscent of 1920 to 1930 auto poster art), and the sponsors' generous budgets. Under contract with several vintage racing associations, Simon traveled to meets all over the United States, many of which required their own Simon poster designs.

Auction ads he created for Rick Cole Auctions on the West Coast gave Simon's work its widest exposure and earned him the title "king of automotive-poster illustrators," used by *Road & Track* magazine in an advertisement for Dennis Simon neckties. These breakthrough designs led to illustration assignments from *Victory Lane*, *Vintage Motorsport*, and *Sports Car International* magazines. Soon, Simon found himself the subject of a one-person art show in England.

In the course of his endeavors, Simon has the well-deserved pleasure of traveling worldwide on artistic assignments. He also spends a lot of studio time completing his commissions. He has an enviable job—doing what he loves, getting paid, and traveling the hemispheres to do it.

With his artistic presence firmly established through vintage racing, Simon is moving to more mainstream auto art through his own company. He uses his "neovintage style" (again, a *Road & Track* description) to design posters, neckwear—even vintage-related shopping bags and sweatshirts.

Simon's auto neckties are spectacular. You can tie on the grille of a Mercedes 540K, a quintet of red racing Ferraris, or a passel of Porsches. Wearing the tie with two open-cockpit racers careening through the streets in the Monaco Grand Prix is a lot safer than driving the course, but it does impart the thrill of this preeminent auto race.

Fine Artist or Painter

Dale Klee offers over a score of signed and numbered prints for sale through his Wyoming, Minnesota, studio. His paintings share a primary subject—old, abandoned automobiles, often with buildings of similar or greater age. "You paint what you know," said Klee of his specialty.

One painting features tattered 1934 and 1939 Fords hulking in the undisturbed snow surrounding a deserted trading post. A huge collection of junked Fords is the theme of *Ace Auto Parts*. His *Old Rivals* shows the faded hulks of two 1937 stock cars, Ford and Chevy, sitting nose-to-nose in front of an abandoned country racetrack.

One would think from these descriptions that Klee's pictures depicting the disintegration of once-proud cars and once-used barns, racetracks, and garages would be "downers," but the effect is quite the reverse.

Klee's artistic style is heightened realism. In it, angles are a bit more angular than in life; colors, shadows, and textures are slightly more pronounced. The russet tones of dry grass, rust under paint, and unpainted barn wood are Klee hallmarks. The effect is a startling power, reminiscent of 1930 to 1950 American illustration. This is not surprising—it is the automotive period Klee most admires. And rural America of that era is the place he likes to capture in his paintings.

"My Dad ran the Standard Oil station in Houghton, Michigan, when I was a kid," he recalled. "I worked there. I had to stand on a stool to reach the windshields of those big cars. I formed my admiration for them then, and I have it to this day."

As he was growing up, Klee roamed midwestern country roads in search of old cars that a young man could afford to buy. (He still does.) "Country people save them to fix up someday—but the 'someday' never comes. I remember finding a 1933 Ford three-window coupe. My knees started shaking when I saw it. But it was a long time before I developed the talent I needed to put old cars and old countryside together."

Klee spent ten years in quality control for a beer can manufacturer and several more as a West Coast aircraft assembler. He has no formal art training but developed his style by collecting and studying second-hand art instruction books, an interest he still pursues. All this time, he has continued to scout rural roads and villages for their 1920s and 1930s buildings and the 1930 to 1950 cars that belong with them. Now, from a trove of photos, sketches, and memories, he creates his unique scenes on canvas. From the originals, he produces prints in editions ranging from 450 to 2,000 at prices from $45 to $65. For an original Klee painting, expect to pay more than $1,000.

"I got started in 1990 with a painting called *Junk Pile* that I did as a joke—a teetering collection of junk cars and parts going straight up in the air. I sold the painting, but so many people asked about it that I had to buy it back and have prints made from it. I then did two other prints. They sold out within a year.

"I advertise in *Hemmings Motor News* and *Street Rodder* magazine, and I've been lucky with publicity. When I get time—which I don't have much of anymore—I go to auto shows. I like talking to car people and customers. It gives me a good perspective on my work."

Klee keeps a computerized database of previous buyers and sends them brochures showing new prints added to the growing stock. The list, which included about five hundred buyers in 1990, now exceeds four thousand. His customers come from all over the world.

When he decided to paint *Old Rivals,* with its ancient, weed-infested, slab-sided country racetrack, Klee traveled more than three hundred miles to photograph the real thing. He arrived home after clicking off a whole roll of film only to find he had never loaded the camera. "I made a lot of sketches from memory real fast!" he said. "As a result, I got more drama into the old place than if I'd had my photos to work from. The old cars I paint had such style. Their lines were beautiful, and there was great attention to detail back then. I can't quite tell you what I feel when I see an abandoned one." Dale Klee does not need words—his canvases telegraph his emotions.

Gallery Operator

Finally, art dealers and art gallery operators market the automotive art of others. Rare is the gallery devoted entirely to automobilia; operating a general-interest art gallery is difficult enough. Career prerequisites include a thorough understanding of automotive art history, strong promotional instincts, a sharp mind for math—and an affluent location.

Additional Resources

Auto Art Magazine
25612 Northeast Colbern Road
Lee's Summit, MO 64086
www.autoartmagazine.com

Art Car Museum
140 Heights Boulevard
Houston, TX 77007
www.artcarmuseum.com
> *This fascinating museum merges autos and art and it serves as a forum for local, national, and international artists. Its emphasis is on art cars, other fine arts, and artists that are rarely, if ever, acknowledged by other cultural institutions.*

Jobs with Automotive Photography

I n addition to automotive still photographer, other careers in automotive photography include assistant, location scout, stylist, and videographer or cinematographer.

Commercial photographers are those who take pictures for advertisements, for sale to stock photo houses or photo rental agencies, and for similar assignments. They may do occasional auto photography. Bob Giandomenico of Collingswood, New Jersey, has converted the one-time Collingswood Theater into a photo studio large enough to take auto studio shots. He has done considerable work for Subaru of America, but Bob is a generalist, not an automotive photographer. He tackles everything from tabletop product pictures to location photography—whatever the job entails.

Those who do a good bit of automotive still photography do it in three overlapping contexts. First come beauty shots, indoors or out. These are most often used as calendar pictures, advertising shots, and poster art. Second are action photos taken during races. These might become part of a photo essay of action and still pictures taken for a car magazine's road tests and new-car reviews. Action film or video represents a third career area that can involve autos, most often for television commercials. Such videographers or cinematographers may also be generalists, shooting new cars one day and a fashion show the next.

Automotive publications may have staff photographers, but the majority work with freelancers. Aspiring photographers, automotive and otherwise, often begin as photographers' assistants.

Photography Assistant

You may attend a school of photography or take photography or cinematography courses in college, but the job is truly learned in the studio and on location. Just as a medical assistant may do everything for a patient except prescribe and diagnose, the photographer's assistant sometimes does everything related to a studio or location "shoot" except operate the camera. Often, experienced assistants do the photography as well. The assistant is expected to arrange the background drapes, rig flood or flash lighting, load cameras, set up props—or pack everything needed for a location session into the studio's van, then perform all the set-up chores once the crew reaches the location.

Automotive Photographer

"I've always liked automobiles, motorcycles, and aircraft, but I went to college to study industrial and commercial photography," says David Dewhurst, a freelance photographer who often completes assignments for *Car & Driver* magazine, along with many other clients.

"When I came out of college in 1970, I couldn't find industrial-commercial work, so I went with a newspaper as a photographer. I persuaded the newspaper owners to run a cycling publication called *Trials & Motocross News,* and I became a photographer-writer for them. That, in turn, led to an offer from *Cycle Guide* in the United States, where I worked as technical editor."

In that job, Dewhurst did a lot of photography and writing. "In my experience, it's not whom you know that counts, but whom you get to know—the contacts you make mean everything. My work at *Cycle Guide* gave me a chance to do a freelance photo essay for *Car & Driver* in 1983—a road test of the Mitsubishi Galant. It has been an excellent client ever since."

Dewhurst specializes in auto and cycle photography, plus a bit of aircraft work "because you develop a reputation for certain kinds of work, and that's what clients buy. In my case, it's based on knowing, understanding, and appreciating the vehicles."

He pointed out that once you learn the essential skills of photography—what to do—that part of an assignment is relatively easy. The hard part is setting the stage in which to shoot the assignment most effectively. They say of real estate, "location, location, location," but that's equally true in the world of automotive photography.

"I scout 95 percent to 98 percent of my own locations and usually set the rules for the shoot," Dewhurst explains. Only for a magazine cover does an art director get involved in creating the picture. Dewhurst looks for locations that aren't hackneyed and that he can use without being run off the land and that involve reasonable location fees, if any. "Location fees are part of my expenses, and freelance magazine assignments don't allow for really high location fees."

Occasionally, he'll use a location scout, which is a related career for an auto enthusiast. The good location scouts who also know cars have a better ability to pick locations than those who don't share an automotive interest.

When asked how many automotive photos he had taken in his twenty-seven-year career, Dewhurst described his two studio walls: each is ten shelves high and forty feet long and filled with three-inch ring binders full of photos.

Dewhurst is now marketing his earlier work as stock photographs for publications such as the *Washington Post,* the *New York Times,* and others needing images of autos (especially cars of a few years back) and road scenes. This work, as well as constant assignments, keeps this automotive photographer very busy.

Stylist

There are several kinds of stylists. Some may make up models, while others prepare foods for studio photographs. In an automotive context, a stylist is responsible for many of the details of an auto advertising still shot or TV spot, including (but not limited to) the models' wardrobes and make-up and, to some extent, the hue and intensity of lighting needed to establish a given mood.

Videographer or Cinematographer

Racing and motorsports filming or videography requires camera people adept in tracking the action, neither leading nor following the moving cars, often with the extra precision demanded by zoom lenses. A massive event such as the Indy 500 or the Twenty-Four Hours of Daytona calls for many camera people, plus a large support staff of video on- and off-line editors and assistant directors, all headed by a director. Motorsports video and television projects also have producers and their support staff who are responsible for the overall production, including securing advertisers, and, in the case of a motorsports video, marketing the completed product.

An example, "My Classic Car," hosted by Dennis Gage, went from pilot status to a regular series on the Nashville Network (now the National Network), which aired many other motorsports events. Each half-hour video magazine covered at least three subjects of interest to car buffs. One of the episodes took viewers inside the Auburn-Cord-Duesenberg Museum, the only auto museum in America housed in an auto company's one-time factory showroom. Viewers were also treated to a look at a Kruse Auction, a complete review of the Chrysler hemi engines, and both historical and contemporary footage of the "Super Snake," the only Mustang that Carroll Shelby ever built with a pure 427 racing engine.

Additional Resources

American Society of Media Photographers
150 North Second Street
Philadelphia, PA 19106
www.asmp.org

> *The American Society of Media Photographers promotes pho-*
> *tographers' rights and educates them about business practices.*
> *This is a great networking forum.*

International Motor Press Association
4 Park Street
Harrington Park, NJ 07640
www.impa.org

> *Membership includes journalists from all media and public relations*
> *specialists.*

Photographer's Market
Writer's Digest Books
F&W Publications
1507 Dana Avenue
Cincinnati, OH 45207

> *This annual directory provides an invaluable resource for*
> *photographers looking to sell their work. In addition to more than*
> *two thousand potential buyers, the book contains a wealth of tips on*
> *all aspects of professional photography.*

CHAPTER FIFTEEN

Careers for Wordsmiths

B ooks, literature, and the automobile have long enjoyed a kinship. An owner's manual accompanies every new car, a custom going back to motoring's early days. There is naturally a big business in out-of-print vintage car manuals and other literature as well. The auto has been and continues to be the subject of hundreds of new book titles every year. From how-to guides to coffee table extravaganzas, the stream of publications seems endless.

What is an automotive writer? A huge variety of people can legitimately claim the title. Some are writers who happen to cover automotive subjects. Others are automotive specialists who happen to write. A rare few are writers who have committed themselves totally to the automobile.

People who compile auto parts catalogs and prepare new car owners' manuals are as much automotive writers as those who review new cars for local newspapers, but they may not dote on cars. The people who report auto industry trends in financial journals may or may not like cars, either, but those who road test cars and report on the latest offerings for national magazines surely do. In the magazine field, some writers are publication employees; most are freelance journalists. The auto racing publicity staff—whether writing for a racing team, sanctioning body, or speedway—must be able to communicate to many media in ways that draw crowds.

Auto writing includes the advertising agency person who blends originality, creativity, and marketing savvy in new car ads and television commercials. The person who compiles newspaper copy for Honest Abe's Wheel-O-Rama qualifies. So does the specialist who devotes a book to the history of salt-flats racing, a rebuilding of the flathead Ford V-8 of the 1930s, or how to do tuck-and-roll upholstery. Even the volunteer editor of a car club's newsletter is an auto writer. However, for career purposes, it helps to get paid.

Earnings in the field of auto writing equal those of other writers. The newspaper auto writer earns the same pay as any other reporter with similar skills. An auto-related book contract has terms similar to those signed by authors of similar books in other categories.

Contrary to what some might think, writing—automotive or otherwise—is anything but glamorous. What one writer called "making words behave" is hard, usually solitary, work. But it helps to like your subject.

Advertising and Marketing Writer

Shortly after graduating from college, Dick Lee took a position at an ad agency that had automotive accounts, but as a cub writer he didn't get them. There he gained experience writing advertising copy and eventually landed another job at a small agency with a lot of local car dealers as clients, and so became an automotive writer. Writing was local at first, then national. The agency's specialty became preparing sales promotion materials and marketing programs for every part of a Ford dealer's business. This was done through the marketing departments of Ford, including the new car, used car, truck, parts and service, and leasing departments, which led to some substantial travel on Lee's part, commuting from Philadelphia to Detroit every week.

Lee says the name of the game was speed. "We were to Ford's huge ad agency as the nit is to the hide of an elephant," adding that his firm's small size gave them greater agility than some of the competition. "Our 'team' (two, or sometimes just me) would come back to Ford's executives with a marketing solution before the big agency could even consider the problem. The Ford people needed us—and ours was an area the big agency just couldn't handle."

This led Lee to a dozen years of hectic airborne commuting and overnight problem solving. Next came three years of writing the ads for Carroll Shelby's Cobra and Shelby Mustangs, plus all the Ford projects. "Same routine," he says, with West Coast flights thrown in. Of course, the cars were great—and the atmosphere, electric."

After "too many years of dragging through airports at night," Lee rejoined Gray & Rogers, the agency he had worked with before. Among other accounts, he was the creative writer for Utica Tools, Castrol Oils, Raybestos Manhattan (brake linings and parts), and Pocono International Raceway. During these years and later, he and his wife fed a growing auto enthusiasm with imported sports cars. Following a road rally accident, they prudently switched to slower-moving classics. He did unpaid writing for the Lincoln Continental Owner's Club (four years as editor of the club's national publication, *Continental Comments*) and for the newsletter of the Delaware Valley Region of the Classic Car Club of America.

Auto writing, whether it's ads or sales promotion programs, showroom literature or catalogs, involves much more reading than writing. If you're writing promotional literature, you have to know what the competition is thinking and saying, so you can take a different sales position. You have to get all the corporate marketing data you can to position your car or your aftermarket (after-the-sale) product or service. You also have to play the "If I were a Spitfire V8, what would I say about myself?" game. In addition, you really need to have a love of the automobile.

"Anybody who calls himself or herself an automotive writer must know the lingo," Lee says. "You don't need to use an obviously 'in' style, but you'd better know the terminology. You're writing to partisans, even if they're not enthusiasts, and they can spot an automotive ignoramus a mile away."

. . . .

Book Author

To get an idea of how vast and complex this subject is, look for the Classic Motorbooks ad in almost any auto enthusiast magazine. It consumes several pages in each issue of *Hemmings Motor News.* The titles show an astonishing range—from *Bubblecars and Microcars* to *90 Years of Ford*, from *Illustrated Ducati Buyers Guide* to *Gas Station Collectibles Price Guide*. Most auto books use photos and text to carry the message.

The titles make something else clear: the vast majority of auto-related books are written by people who are subject specialists. Tightly focused interest, such as knowing the matching numbers for Pontiac GTOs, and a willingness to research a given topic to the smallest nut and bolt are the hallmarks of most auto book authors.

Writing skills used to be secondary to information, but no longer; now they are necessary. Although publishers have copy editors who review a manuscript and make it more readable, they may instead tell the author what areas need smoothing. If getting an auto book published is your goal, sloppy writing is not the path to victory. Be clear. Be precise. Avoid clumsy phrases. Use short words (write "also," not "in addition to").

It doesn't pay to invest time in writing your book until a publisher expresses interest. To reach this point, the best route is a proposal. It should include a marketing rationale for your book, a full outline of all chapters, and at least one complete chapter to show your writing skills, subject knowledge, and ability to organize. Include a few sample photographs to demonstrate photo quality.

The best ways to find automotive publishers are to:

1. Explore *Writer's Market*, a guidebook you can either find in your library or buy (Writers Digest Books, Cincinnati, OH).
2. Look for the publishers of recent auto book titles similar to yours in a bookstore or library.

3. Buy a book or two in the format or subject closest to what you have in mind from either a bookstore or a mail-order company such as Classic Motorbooks. Classic Motorbooks' parent company, Motorbooks International, is a book publisher as well as a marketer.

Automotive books are for a specialized market. Since they are not blockbuster sellers, they wouldn't interest a literary agent. This is just as well, since the agent takes a 10 to 15 percent commission. Payment is usually by royalties, which are anywhere from about 3 to 8 percent of the cover price or wholesale (net) price and are based on copies sold. Advances—money paid to you against eventual royalty sales—will not be large sums. Don't expect the publisher to bankroll your manuscript preparation time or photography costs.

When you've had your proposal accepted, you will be asked to sign a contract setting forth the publisher's terms. It indicates whether you are to supply photos and if you'll be paid extra for them. The royalty terms, book length, and manuscript due date are also written out. These terms are somewhat negotiable—but only before you sign the contract.

Although you probably won't get rich, you'll have the joy of seeing your "baby" arrive, its words and pictures tucked between covers, anywhere from nine months to two years after you finish writing the book.

Magazine Writer

The magazine writer usually has one type of writing he or she does best. It may be writing car-related, humorous reminiscences or expressing in words his or her opinion of a given vehicle. It could be straight racing reportage. But no matter what a writer's specialty eventually becomes, one of the only ways to enter this field is to try your hand at an unsolicited article. In the case of a magazine, your manuscript will no doubt languish on a "slush pile" for weeks before being read and acknowledged. (If you want your manuscript returned if it's not purchased, you must enclose a stamped, self-addressed envelope.) If a magazine accepts your item, and you have more you could write in subsequent articles, you can use your one acceptance to establish a rapport with a staff editor in the hope of selling future articles.

A good resource for finding auto-related magazines is the *Writer's Market,* published annually. Each magazine listed includes guidelines for submission of materials. Almost without exception, unsolicited manuscripts are neither acknowledged nor returned unless accompanied by sufficient return postage. The same rule applies to book publishers. Best suggestion in any case: query before submitting material.

There is no other way to enter magazine writing unless you launch your own publication. All subsequent opportunities will come through this first open door: continuing freelance assignments; jobs from other magazines (based on the fact you have written for XYZ Journal); even joining a magazine staff in a salaried job as a staff writer or, eventually, an editor.

Many people assume that editors were writers first. Some have written before and many have not. Editors have a talent for pruning and sharpening the words of others with a mixture of skill, objectivity, and subject knowledge. This last trait is especially true of automotive editors—they must truly know and love the subject.

Newspaper Writer

In newspapers, you will likely begin by asking a local newspaper editor for a low-paid assignment or one that could be written for free to gain experience. Be persistent. Your completed assignment will earn a speedy yes, no, or yes-with-rewrite response from your editor. Save a copy of everything you write that is published—no matter how inconsequential you may think it. With these samples, or clips, you can show what you have done. If you have journalism experience or a degree in journalism or English, you might land a newspaper job. If it is not automotive, it is employment, so be grateful. Al Haas of the *Philadelphia Inquirer* covered the city life and entertainment beats for years before becoming the paper's automotive writer. And if you wind up writing restaurant reviews instead of road tests, at least you will be writing with a full stomach and a paycheck.

Racing Journalist

Diana Smartt disproves the notion that all automotive journalists are men. But she entered this once-male field in an unorthodox manner.

A librarian in Hatboro, Pennsylvania, Smartt decided that she wanted to write on the side. She approached her local newspaper, the *Hatboro Public Spirit*. The editor said she could work for the paper if she could find subjects of general interest.

Smartt responded to this mandate easily by choosing auto racing because a college friend had married Al Holbert, a fast-rising national racing star. A local Porsche dealer, Holbert had been a protégé of Roger Penske and was a strong competitor. The budding journalist received her editor's OK to profile Holbert. Her editor insisted the article also include some technical aspects of auto racing, and it ran in the paper's sports pages. She has stayed in this field ever since. From time to time, she also covers equestrian events and professional football, and she has since written several magazine articles on auto racing.

Although Smartt was new to the finer points of the racing and automotive world, her father had fired her interest in motorsports as a child. "He introduced me to the excitement of the Sebring road races and the Indy 500. I shared his love of the smell of hot racing oil and the deafening roar of sleek, taut race cars taking to the track."

How did she conquer the terminology of this intensely technical world? "I am a quick study," she says. "I learned about air-cooled engines, emergency fiberglass fabrication at trackside, and the rules of different racing classes—engine displacement limits and other requirements. Fortunately, it came easily to me."

As a distant observer, Smartt had watched Al Holbert and his racing team win at Le Mans, Daytona, and Sebring during the 1985–86 racing seasons. She tackled her first Holbert interview by phone. A meeting at the Holbert Racing garage behind the dealership followed. Holbert, though involved with a million details, was gracious with his time. Other stories followed as Al Holbert became the leading record holder on the IMSA Camel GTP circuit, and as his team designed and built the Quaker State March Porsche Indy 500 contender. As director of Porsche Motorsport North America, Holbert managed the team.

Through covering Holbert's career, Smartt became part of auto racing's reportorial elite. She attended races (at times in the pits), met other famous racing drivers, was part of their racing banquets, and hobnobbed with their wives.

"The racing world is like a tent circus," Smartt observes. "You set up, race, then break down and travel on." She often tries for interviews when the "tent" goes up because everyone scatters at race's end like the trails of dust they boiled up on the course.

Press people often try to approach drivers in the hectic half hour just before a race. Often, this may be their first chance to get a statement, but the drivers are nervous and tightly focused— more interested in engine dynamics than a dynamic interview.

As a female automotive journalist, Smartt feels that her membership in American Women in the Sports Media defines her. In a world that once was largely closed to women, she is glad for this validation, but she has validation of her own: for the past several years, she has been the only woman reporter at most IMSA races.

Book Buyer, Salesperson, or Dealer

In the world of bookselling, individual and chain bookstores employ buyers who evaluate new auto-related books just as they do those on every other subject. Book buyers select the titles for their store shelves from among those touted by book salespeople. These buyers are not necessarily auto buffs, although they could be. A car buff book buyer would presumably exercise more informed purchasing judgment in that subject area than someone who doesn't know much about cars.

Motorbooks International of Osceola, Wisconsin, is arguably the nation's largest direct-mail retailer of motoring books through its Classic Motorbooks catalog. For many years, Brad Siqueiros has been the firm's book buyer for both the retail catalog sales and of books that Motorbooks International wholesales to other bookstores.

As the buyer for this large organization, Siqueiros's job is to review the nearly two thousand new titles available each year in the automotive, aviation, and military history fields, the three areas in which the company specializes. He has the help of others, including Bill Krause, the firm's retail sales director.

As a book buyer, you must develop a critical sense of what would be right for your audience. Says Krause, "Naturally, we can't accept every auto book that's out there, so we rely on a combination of the quality of a given book and the popularity of related titles with our bookstore and mail-order audiences to decide whether or not to list it.

"Even though I've been buying books for both our retail and wholesale departments for several years, it continues to amaze me how many books there are being published on what outsiders think of as a specialized market—the automobile." Automotive publishing is truly international, with sales of Motorbooks titles coming from all over the world. It seems there are no boundaries to auto enthusiasm.

Book buyers usually have a bachelor's degree in English or some type of marketing. Many also have some type of previous publishing or purchasing experience before they obtain a job as an organization's sole buyer. A strong understanding of the specific market and client buying preferences is also very important.

New Book Marketer

In the case of the parent company, Motorbooks International, the United Kingdom connection is natural. Tom Warth, an Englishman, founded the company as Classic Motorbooks in 1965 to sell British sports car magazine subscriptions to Americans. Warth soon saw that books provided a better business focus, and he began scouring the world markets for automotive books to sell by mail. He changed the company name to Motorbooks International when it started wholesaling auto books, and he began publishing volumes on his own.

At the time Tom Warth began publishing auto books, he hired Tim Parker, then editorial director of Osprey Publishing in London, as publishing director. Osprey was a major publisher of titles sold by Classic Motorbooks. Parker came to Motorbooks International to increase its publishing operation, then averaging six to eight books a year.

"I had been with Osprey for seven years," Parker recalls. "My experience also included an earlier seven years with an auto workshop manual publisher and a stint with a firm best known for the title *How to Tune S.U. Carburetors,* required reading for British sports car owners worldwide.

"When I started, auto enthusiasm was almost my sole qualification, and I can't honestly say I'm formally qualified today to do what I do. These days, an auto enthusiast can't make it in publishing on enthusiasm alone; he or she must have at the very least editing skills, computer skills, or marketing skills in the bargain."

His disclaimer notwithstanding, Tim Parker is president and chief executive officer of Motorbooks International. The firm now employs one hundred people, publishes more than a hundred titles a year, produces the definitive auto books catalog, and generates more than $30 million in annual sales.

The Classic Motorbooks catalog is remarkable. It totals about 130 pages, including a core segment that is revised every six months. The catalog also contains from four to sixteen full-color "wrap" (front and back) pages featuring the newest offerings. The catalog contains some forty-five hundred auto books and related items—and several million copies are mailed annually.

Used Auto Literature Dealer

This is a career that can often grow out of collecting. Interest in a particular vehicle can lead to collecting literature on that subject and selling or trading duplicate items to others. This can be turned into a business, buying and reselling auto literature of all kinds. Doing so requires space, organizational skills, and eventually computer capability for inventory control.

Bob Johnson of Framingham, Massachusetts, took a different route to a business that now includes eighty to ninety tons of literature. Hooked on cars in the 1950s through his father's interest, this one-time self-employed business consultant to the Small Business Administration started by buying a collection of old auto parts to resell.

"A friend who had literature for sale looked at these bulky parts and said, 'Bob, why don't you buy my paper [trade term for literature]? It makes more sense in terms of space.' I did, and that was the start."

Bob Johnson shifted his business into high gear with one bold move. He bought the complete auto literature collection from the estate of a New Jersey enthusiast. The collection weighed about sixty tons and filled three tractor-trailers.

In the intervening years, he has seen his paper inventory—and his business—grow tremendously. "Agricultural equipment is a big thing now," Johnson says. "Prices are going up on old tractors and mechanical farm implements—and the paper for that equipment is enjoying a healthy market.

"Paper selling is a pure form of capitalism," Johnson adds. "Car collections come and go. Scads of collector cars change hands every year. New buyers are looking for the paper related to their cars."

A lot of car interest is age related, and tastes for particular models and years of cars change as the tastes of an individual change. Says Johnson, "All of a sudden, he or she wants a brass car—something made prior to 1916 and the advent of electric lights. So the brass market is another growth area.

"That's a wonderful era. There was a lot more art, a lot more care, put into older auto literature. There's great work in a lot of early paper. This business is quantitative. You have to be sensitive to change," Johnson asserts. "You do this by being very much aware of what people want, and then you try to supply that market. Keeping up a supply is key. For instance, business has boomed in the last several months. I have a lot more volume in buying and selling."

Johnson buys paper at auto and memorabilia auctions, where he is among the country's top buyers. He buys collections privately as well and has made purchases from individuals, auto dealers, and even car factories. There are times when buying desirable paper means having to take what isn't so good; paper is often sold in large lots and must be sorted through for the important pieces.

He prefers to buy by telephone. "If I travel, I have to subtract my travel costs from the amount I'm willing to pay. I let the seller know that."

Johnson now has two full-time employees plus a third part-time. He keeps changing his ads in *Hemmings Motor News* and other publications to reflect his latest acquisitions, many one-of-a-kind or rare items.

"When I bought that huge collection in 1986, it was in complete disarray," he recalls. "I organized it and maintain my inventory with my staff, the computer, and my own layers of knowledge. I try to see everything once, when it comes in. That way, I get a feel for it—what a fair price is and how well it might sell. If you touch something, you tend to remember it."

More than 90 percent of Johnson's sales are by phone. He and his staff have phone extensions throughout the warehouse. Relative to the type of literature and its location, a staff member can review the individual piece with a caller without retracing steps to a phone. Bob Johnson or an employee can usually answer a caller's question within three or four minutes.

Obviously, this career involves a very specialized type of dealer who must have a vast amount of knowledge and personal drive to maintain a business such as Bob Johnson's. There is no specific background or degree that might be expected for this niche market, but small business courses and strong computer skills could help prepare a person to start a new business.

Additional Resources

American Journalism Review (AJR)
University of Maryland
1117 Journalism Building
College Park, MD 20742
www.ajr.org

> AJR *publishes exciting features, strong opinions, lively articles, and profiles. Every issue is packed with valuable information, continuing assessment of news and industry issues, and much more.*

Association for Education in Journalism and Mass
  Communications (AEJMC)
234 Outlet Pointe Boulevard
Columbia, SC 29210
www.aejmc.org

> *The AEJMC is a nonprofit, educational association of journalism and mass communication faculty, administrators, students, and media professionals. This respected association could provide you with additional information on finding the education you need to build a foundation for a career in journalism in the automotive industry.*

Association for Women in Sports Media
P.O. Box 726
Farmington, CT 06034
www.aswmonline.org

The Association for Women in Sports Media is an organization of women who work in the sports media and women and men who support them in their work. The website features a job bank and scholarship information.

Writers Market
Writer's Digest Books
F&W Publications
1507 Dana Avenue
Cincinnati, OH 45207
www.writersmarket.com

This annual directory offers tips for getting published, as well as professional advice from agents and editors. WritersMarket.com is a searchable database of more than four thousand publishers and literary agents to whom writers can submit their work. You must subscribe to it for access to the information. Go to your local library for the free book version.

About the Authors

Richard and Mary Price Lee were car buffs even before their marriage. Their wedding trip included a slow climb up and quick drop down New Hampshire's Mount Equinox in a near-brakeless 1948 MG-TC.

For many years, Richard Lee wrote for advertising agencies serving Ford Motor Company and Shelby Automotive, among other car-related accounts. He also edited the Lincoln Continental Owners' Club national magazine and was a regional director of the Classic Car Club of America.

Mary Price Lee taught sixth grade, worked as a book publisher's assistant, and wrote eight coping and career books for high school readers.

Jointly they have since written another dozen such books, including *Opportunities in Animal and Pet Care Careers* for VGM Career Books. All this time, they were trading in sports, classic, and special-interest cars, with more than a score of collectibles passing in and out of their lives.

Richard Lee earned an A.B. in English at the College of William & Mary. Mary Price Lee holds B.A. and M.S. degrees in education from the University of Pennsylvania. The Lees have three grown children and a never-quite-restored 1969 Porsche 912 Targa.